SOCIAL WORK AND CRIMINAL JUSTICE:

VOLUME 6

THE PROCESS AND OUTCOMES OF PROBATION SUPERVISION

r

ry

h Centre
ocial Science
rling

AL RESEARCH UNIT

ACKNOWLEDGEMENTS

Since its inception in the Spring of 1994, this research project has received a great deal of the time, energy, co-operation and enthusiasm of many clients, social workers and managers in the areas which participated in the study.

We would like to acknowledge their support and that received from the Scottish Office Home Department, in particular from Dr Fiona Paterson, Principal Research Officer in the Central Research Unit. We are also grateful for the assistance of the Scottish Criminal Record Office in providing access to data required.

Special thanks are due to Vivien Campbell, freelance researcher, for assisting in the data collection and, in particular, for her perseverance in tracking down respondents in one of the study areas. Thanks also to Pam Lavery and Trish Hughes for their patience in deciphering the endless transcripts, and their tolerance in ignoring some of the more colourful language used - especially by the clients!

Gill McIvor
Monica Barry
1998

SOCIAL WORK AND CRIMINAL JUSTICE
RESEARCH PROGRAMME REPORTS

Paterson, F. and Tombs, J. (1998)   Social Work and Criminal Justice: Volume 1 -

The Impact of Policy. The Stationery Office.

Phase One:

McAra, L. (1998)   Social Work and Criminal Justice: Volume 2 -

Early Arrangements. The Stationery Office.

Phase Two:

Brown, L., Levy, L.   Social Work and Criminal Justice: Volume 3 -

and McIvor, G. (1998)   *The National and Local Context.* The Stationery Office.

Brown, L., Levy, L. (1998)   Social Work and Criminal Justice: Volume 4 -

Sentencer Decision Making. The Stationery Office.

McAra, L. (1998a)   Social Work and Criminal Justice: Volume 5 -

Parole Board Decision Making. The Stationery Office.

McIvor, G. and   Social Work and Criminal Justice: Volume 6 -

Barry, M. (1998)   *Probation.* The Stationery Office.

McIvor, G. and   Social Work and Criminal Justice: Volume 7 -

Barry, M. (1998a)   *Community Based Throughcare.* The Stationery Office

CONTENTS

SUMMARY

INTRODUCTION

The Policy

In Scotland, statutory social work services to offenders and their families are provided by the local authority social work departments. Since April 1991, the Scottish Office has reimbursed to social work departments the full costs of providing a range of statutory social work services in the criminal justice system. National Objectives and Standards (the National Standards) were introduced by the Social Work Services Group of the Scottish Office to coincide with the introduction of the funding initiative.

The National Standards and the funding initiative cover: social enquiry reports; court social work services; probation; community service; and throughcare (social work in prisons is funded by the Scottish Prison Service). Since 1991, the initiative has been extended to supervised release orders, bail information and accommodation schemes, and supervised attendance order schemes (the latter two schemes are not yet available on a national basis).

The main aims of the Government's policy are:

- to reduce the use of custody by increasing the availability, improving the quality and targeting the use of community based court disposals and throughcare services on those most at risk of custody, especially young adult repeat offenders;

- to enable offenders to address their offending behaviour and make a successful adjustment to law abiding life.

Background to the Research

Central Government's review and evaluation of implementation of the funding initiative and the National Standards involves a programme of inspection by Social Work Services Inspectorate (SWSI), interpretation of statistics and a programme of research.

The research programme examines progress towards policy objectives. Four sheriff court areas each in separate social work authorities, were selected as study sites for Phase Two of the research programme to reflect areas of both high and low population density and to represent both specialist and more generic forms of organising social work criminal justice services. The names of the four areas have been anonymised in reports and are referred to as Scott, Wallace, Burns and Bruce.

The present study examines the process and outcomes of probation supervision following the introduction of 100 per cent funding and National Standards. In examining the process and outcomes of probation supervision in Scotland it seeks to describe the characteristics of probationers; to document the services offered by supervising social workers and the framework within which they are provided; and to examine the effectiveness of probation supervision in meeting probationers' needs and reducing the risk of further offending behaviour.

In three of the study authorities - Bruce, Scott and Wallace - the research focused upon probation cases held by two social work teams. In the fourth area - Burns - the focus was upon the work of a single team. The research focused upon probation cases closed between 1 July 1994 and 30 April 1995. Information was obtained, in the main, from social work case files, from questionnaires completed by supervising social workers in individual cases and from interviews with probationers.

CHARACTERISTICS OF THE SAMPLE

The total sample consisted of 155 offenders sentenced to probation across the four study areas. The majority of orders had been imposed by the sheriff court under summary proceedings. Just under half contained additional requirements, with the nature of these requirements tending to reflect the availability of services in the study areas. Eighty-two per cent of probationers were male and just under half were between 16 and 20 years of age. Around half the sample had six or more previous convictions when made subject to probation and just under three-fifths had received their orders for offences involving dishonesty. Thirty-eight per cent of probationers were believed by social enquiry report (SER) authors to have been at risk of a custodial sentence. Family problems, drug and alcohol abuse, and mental health problems featured prominently in SERs. Offending was most often attributed to alcohol or drug abuse, though in a fifth of cases offenders were said to have been motivated by financial gain and in a similar proportion of cases offending was described as opportunistic or impulsive. In recommending probation to the courts, social workers generally referred to the potential offered by probation to address offending behaviour or behaviour associated with offending; to provide help with practical problems or support of a more general kind; or to capitalise upon the offender's motivation to change.

Differences Between Research Sites

Probationers in Bruce were more likely to have been ordained to appear for sentence and were less likely to have received probation for offences involving dishonesty. Bruce contained a higher proportion of female offenders and a slightly lower proportion of young offenders than the other areas. Probationers in Bruce had fewest previous convictions and custodial sentences, were more likely to be first offenders and were less likely to have previous experience of communitybased social work disposals. They were less likely to have been considered by the SER author as being at risk of custody but were more likely to have additional requirements recommended to the court.

By contrast, probationers in Wallace had been sentenced for a higher number of offences, had most previous convictions and had served a higher average number of previous custodial sentences. Wallace contained the lowest proportion of first offenders and the highest proportion of persistent offenders. Probationers in Wallace were most likely to be considered at risk of custody and were most likely to be breached.

Differences Between Types of Offender

Young offenders were more likely than adults to have been recommended for and to receive a probation order with additional requirements, to have been given probation for an offence involving dishonesty, to have been considered at risk of custody and to have been breached. They were more often than adults described in SERs as having family problems and problems related to low educational achievement. Offending by young probationers was more often described as impulsive or opportunistic, as a response to boredom or as having occurred under the influence of offending peers, and they were more likely to be recommended for probation as a means of obtaining help with employment. By contrast, alcohol abuse and medical or mental health problems were more likely to feature among adult offenders and their offending was more likely to be linked to alcohol abuse or emotional pressure. Probation was more likely to be recommended for adults as a means of addressing the abuse of alcohol or drugs.

In comparison with first or early offenders, persistent offenders were more likely to have additional requirements recommended and attached to their probation orders. They were more likely to have been sentenced for a main offence involving dishonesty, were more often considered at risk of custody and were more likely to be breached. Peer group pressure was more often invoked in explanations of offending by first or early offenders and probation was more likely to be recommended for this category of offender as a means of addressing relationship and financial problems. Alcohol and drug abuse more often featured in explanations of offending by persistent offenders and they were more likely to be recommended for probation to address offending behaviour and drug abuse and to access help in relation to housing and general support.

Female probationers were less likely than males to have additional requirements recommended and attached to their orders. They were slightly older than men, less likely to be single and more likely to have dependent children living in the same household. Women had fewer previous convictions, were more often first offenders and were less likely to have previously served a custodial sentence. Whilst men and women were equally likely to have received probation for offences involving dishonesty, women's offences typically involved theft and fraud while men's offences involved housebreaking and car theft. Women were less likely to be breached and were more likely to have their probation orders discharged early on the grounds of satisfactory progress having been made. Women were more often identified as having mental health or emotional problems. Their offending was more likely to be explained in terms of financial gain or as a response to emotional stress, and they were more likely than men to be recommended for probation as a means of accessing support of a general kind. Male probationers were more often described as having problems relating to alcohol abuse. Their offending was more likely to be linked to alcohol, to be described as opportunistic or impulsive or to have been in response to boredom. Probation was more likely to be recommended for male than female probationers to address offending behaviour and alcohol abuse.

THE PROBATION PROCESS

Contacts with Social Workers

The process of probation supervision was examined in 112 cases. The National Standard which stipulates that probationers should first be seen within one week of the order being made was met in 67 per cent of cases; the requirement of at least eight contacts in the first three months was met in 44 per cent of cases; that requiring at least two home visits in the first three months in 47 per cent of cases; and the timing of initial reviews in 51 per cent of cases. With the exception of home visits, the standards were consistently less often met in Bruce than in the other study areas. The lower number of reviews in Wallace appeared to be attributable to the higher percentage of breached orders in that area.

Action Plans

Services Offered

Action plans were present in all but three probation case files. Offending behaviour, personal relationships and employment featured most often in action plans and in the services offered to probationers. The majority of services were delivered on an individual basis and most were provided by the supervising social worker. Other individuals or agencies were most likely to be involved in the provision of services relating to employment, alcohol, drugs and health issues. The objectives most often identified in case files focused upon offending, employment, alcohol and drugs. Action plans and services provided varied according to the characteristics of probationers.

Differences Between Research Sites

The areas of work identified in action plans and the services provided to probationers varied across the research areas. Action plans and services provided to offenders in Bruce were less likely to include reference to offending behaviour, alcohol abuse or financial problems and were more likely to focus upon relationships, use of leisure time and physical or mental health.

The primary objectives and services provided to probationers in Scott more often addressed offending behaviour, drug and alcohol use, financial problems and social skills.

Action plans in Wallace were least likely to include reference to the probationer's use of leisure time, and work undertaken with probationers in this area was less likely to focus upon accommodation, employment and drugs. The primary objectives in work with probationers in Wallace were broadly similar to those in Scott, focusing on offending, employment, alcohol and drugs. The apparent mismatch between probation objectives and services provided in Wallace is likely to be attributable to the high breach rate which prevented much work from being undertaken in a significant proportion of cases.

THE OUTCOMES OF PROBATION

Around three-fifths of objectives appeared to have been achieved in full or to a significant degree though this was true of only 14 per cent of objectives identified in respect of probationers who were breached. Objectives relating to offending behaviour appeared to have been achieved completely or to a significant extent in 56 per cent of cases; those relating to employment or accommodation appeared least often to have been achieved. Objectives were less likely to have been achieved in Wallace (43 per cent) than in Bruce (69 per cent) or Scott (71 per cent), but this was attributable to the higher proportion of breaches in that area. With breaches excluded, objectives appeared more often to have been achieved in Scott (85 per cent) than in Bruce (68 per cent) or Wallace (69 per cent).

Probation objectives were more often achieved in full or to a significant extent with adult offenders, though much of this difference could be accounted for by the higher proportion of young offenders who were breached. Objectives were more likely to be achieved with first or early offenders than with persistent offenders even when 'successful' orders alone were considered. When successful orders alone were considered, objectives were more often achieved in whole or to a significant degree in respect of probationers sentenced for offences involving dishonesty. Objectives were more often achieved with female probationers, this difference being accounted for partly, but not entirely, by the lower breach rate among women.

Fifty-nine per cent of orders were completed in full, 14 per cent were discharged early and 25 per cent were breached. The highest breach rate and the highest proportions of probationers who received one or more formal warnings were found in Wallace, while probation orders in Bruce were more likely than in the other areas to have been terminated through an application for early discharge. Just under half the breach applications resulted from the probationer's conviction for a further offence and just over half of all breaches resulted in the imposition of a custodial sentence. Overall, just under a third of probationers were convicted of or charged with a further offence while on probation: the proportion was highest in Wallace and identical in Bruce and Scott, despite the fact that probationers in Scott might have been assumed, on the basis of their previous criminal histories, to present a higher risk of re-offending than in Bruce.

SOCIAL WORKERS' VIEWS OF THE EFFECTIVENESS OF PROBATION

Objectives

Addressing offending and drug use, providing the probationer with practical support, getting the probationer through the order and addressing attitudes or behaviour associated with offending were the objectives of supervision most commonly identified by social workers in the 98 cases for which questionnaires were completed. The greatest progress was thought to be made towards achieving objectives concerned with personal relationships, offending and successful completion of the order. Around a third of probationers were said to have been very motivated to address their offending and just over a quarter were thought highly motivated to address other problems. Three-fifths of probationers were said to have responded positively to probation.

Likelihood of Re-offending

Forty per cent of probationers were considered unlikely to re-offend while in 17 per cent of cases re-offending was thought very likely. Perceived risk of re-offending was inversely related to probationers' motivation, their response to probation and the extent to which offending related objectives had been achieved. Probationers were assessed as very likely to re-offend because their attitudes, behaviour or circumstances were unchanged. In discussing probationers who were considered unlikely to re-offend, social workers made reference to their motivation to avoid further offending, improvements or stability in their personal circumstances and the acquisition of personal skills.

Just under three-quarters of probationers were considered less likely to re-offend since being placed on probation. Probation was believed to have had some positive impact upon the risk of re-offending in 68 per cent of cases in the sample.

Differences Between Research Sites

The objectives identified by social workers varied across the research sites. Probation objectives were least likely to be achieved in Wallace and probationers in Wallace were more often thought than in other areas to present a continued risk of re-offending.

Probationers in Bruce were less likely to be considered at risk of further offending and were more likely to be said to have demonstrated a reduction in risk while subject to probation than other areas. Social workers in Bruce appeared to place as much emphasis upon offending behaviour than did those in the other study areas even though offending featured less often in this area in the reasons for recommending probation, in action plans, in the services provided to probationers and in the objectives derived from an analysis of case files. The pattern of findings suggests that tackling offending may often have been an implicit objective in Bruce, which was addressed indirectly through attention to other areas.

Differences Between Types of Offender

Young offenders were considered to have been less motivated to address their offending and other problems and less likely to have shown a positive response to probation. They were more often thought to present a risk of continued offending and were less likely to have demonstrated a reduction in risk of re-offending since being made subject to probation.

Probation objectives were less likely to have been achieved with persistent offenders, who were more often thought not to have been motivated to address their offending and other problems. Persistent offenders were less often said to have demonstrated a positive response to probation and were more often thought to present a risk of continued offending. Persistent offenders were, however, equally likely to have shown a reduced risk of re-offending since being placed on probation.

Women were more often said to have been motivated to address their offending behaviour and other problems and were more often thought to have shown a positive response to probation supervision while men were considered more likely to re-offend. These differences appeared, however, to be attributable to the differing characteristics of male and female probationers in the sample.

PROBATIONERS' EXPERIENCES AND VIEWS OF PROBATION

Objectives of the Order and Motivation

Most of the 65 probationers who were interviewed recognised that one of the main purposes of probation was to address offending behaviour and just over half suggested that it was also intended to provide help with problems. The majority stressed the importance of being motivated to change and willing to contribute to the process for probation to be effective. Most probationers were unclear about the existence of an action plan, though they were aware of what the social worker considered to be the main issues in the case and were generally in accordance with the social worker's definition of the problem areas to be addressed. Offending behaviour and drug or alcohol problems were most often mentioned by probationers as areas which should be worked on during probation. Three-quarters of probationers indicated that they had been motivated to address their problems when placed on probation; however, in agreement with social workers' views, younger offenders were less likely than adult probationers to be motivated in this respect.

Content of Supervision

Just under half the probationers thought that the length of their order had been about right while a third believed it to have been too long. Most believed that the frequency of contact with their social worker was about right though a few would have preferred more or less frequent contact, depending upon their circumstances. Probationers identified help with practical or emotional problems, having someone to talk to and referral to/liaison with other agencies as of most benefit to them. Most believed that the help they received from their social workers was adequate though two-fifths would have valued additional help of a practical or supportive kind. The features of probation which probationers found least helpful were the location or frequency of appointments and the possibility of breach. The relationship established with the social worker appeared to be a significant aspect of probation supervision. Those features of the social worker's approach which probationers found most helpful were openness and approachability combined with an ability to influence circumstances and help the probationer to better understand his/her situation and behaviour.

When asked what they had hoped to achieve while on probation, probationers most often cited avoidance of further offending (in just under three-fifths of cases) followed by employment/education, addressing drug use, obtaining a more stable lifestyle, personal development, addressing alcohol use and accommodation. The majority of probationers reported that they had discussed offending behaviour in some detail during their probation order. Those who had attended probation groups or intensive probation programmes generally found such approaches to be stimulating and challenging.

Risk of Re-offending

Most probationers believed that it was unlikely that they would re-offend, though further offending was thought more likely by younger probationers. Compared with when they were placed on probation, over three-quarters of probationers considered themselves to be less at risk of re-offending and the majority of this group believed that probation had played some part in reducing this risk. Other factors which were said to have impacted positively upon their risk of re-offending included their own motivation to avoid offending and its consequences and improvements in their personal circumstances.

Overall, most probationers believed that their experience on probation had been worthwhile. While a quarter thought that they had gained nothing from probation, the remainder cited benefits such as resolving their problems, gaining self confidence, motivation or self respect, learning self control and having 'time out' to reflect on or change their situation. Some wanted not just supervision but an element of control to provide structure in their lives which had been absent in the past.

CONCLUSION

There were area differences in policy implementation which, it is suggested, could be attributable to organisational factors at the local level. More specifically, National Standards were least often met in Bruce, there was less evidence of clear targeting and gate-keeping and probation practice appeared more closely aligned to a traditional welfare model which places greater emphasis upon probationers' problems and less on their offending behaviour. This, it is suggested, may have resulted from the existence of generic management arrangements and the absence of systematic monitoring in that area.

It is concluded that the research presents a generally optimistic picture of probation practice in Scotland. The framework provided by the National Standards appears on the whole to provide an appropriate structure within which offending behaviour and other issues can be addressed. The policy initiative appears to have succeeded in large measure in re-focusing probation practice such as to enhance its emphasis upon tackling offending behaviour and in so doing increase the effectiveness, in the short term at least, of probation supervision. Some managers, however, believed that further progress could still be made in relation to the development of more imaginative approaches to work with probationers, including the use of groupwork and modular programmes, especially with younger offenders with whom probation appeared to be less effective.

CHAPTER ONE

INTRODUCTION AND METHODOLOGY

INTRODUCTION

In Scotland, statutory social work services to offenders and their families are provided by the local authority social work departments. Since April 1991, the Scottish Office has reimbursed to social work departments the full costs of providing a range of statutory social work services in the criminal justice system. National Objectives and Standards (the National Standards) were introduced by the Social Work Services Group of the Scottish Office to coincide with the introduction of the funding initiative. The aim of the National Standards is to promote the development of high quality management and practice, the most efficient and effective use of resources and to provide social work services to the criminal justice system which have the confidence of both the courts and the wider public.

The National Standards and the funding initiative cover: social enquiry reports; court social work services; probation; community service[1]; and throughcare (social work in prisons is funded by the Scottish Prison Service). Since 1991, the initiative has been extended to supervised release orders, bail information and accommodation schemes, and supervised attendance order schemes (the latter two schemes are not available on a national basis). It is intended to include diversion from prosecution in the 100 per cent funding arrangement, subject to the progress of pilot schemes established in 1996. At present, fine supervision, means enquiry reports and deferred sentence supervision are not included in the funding initiative.

Prior to the introduction of the 100 per cent funding initiative and the National Standards, local authorities had to fund the majority of social work services out of their general income. Criminal justice services were, therefore, in competition for resources with other local authority services and as a result were not always of sufficient quantity and quality to meet the requirements of the courts.

The main aims of the Government's policy are[2]:

- to reduce the use of custody by increasing the availability, improving the quality and targeting the use of community based court disposals and throughcare services on those most at risk of custody, especially young adult repeat offenders;

- to enable offenders to address their offending behaviour and make a successful adjustment to law abiding life.

BACKGROUND TO THE RESEARCH

Central Government's review and evaluation of implementation of the funding initiative and the National Standards involves a programme of inspection by Social Work Services Inspectorate (SWSI), interpretation of statistics and a programme of research.

The research programme is being conducted in three phases. The main purpose of Phase One, which was undertaken in 1992-1993, was to examine the responses of key criminal justice decision makers and Scottish Office officials to the principal objectives of the policy and the early arrangements for its implementation (McAra, 1998). Phase Two (of which this study is a part) consists of five inter-related studies, conducted in 1994-1995, which examine progress towards policy objectives: the national and local context of policy implementation (Brown, Levy and McIvor, 1998); sentencer decision making (Brown and Levy, 1998); Parole Board decision making ((McAra, 1998a); the process and outcomes of probation (McIvor and Barry, 1998); and the process and outcomes of throughcare (McIvor and Barry, 1998a). Phase Three will look at the longer term impact of services for offenders.

Four sheriff court areas, each in separate social work authorities, were selected as study sites for the research programme to reflect areas of both high and low population density and to represent both specialist and more generic forms of organising social work criminal justice services. The names of the four areas have been anonymised in reports and are referred to as Scott, Wallace, Burns and Bruce.

The National Standards (SWSG, 1991, paras. 12.1-4) define the key objectives of social work practice in the criminal justice system as being:

---

[1] The 100 % funding initiative and National Objectives and Standards were first applied to community service in 1989.

[2] Evaluation Strategy Working Group, September 1990. More recent statements (the 1996 White Paper on Crime and Punishment, paragraphs 9.1 and 10.3) are consistent with these aims.

- to enable a reduction in the incidence of custody, whether on remand, at sentence, or in default of a financial penalty, where it is used for lack of a suitable, available community based social work disposal;

- to promote and enhance the range and quality of community based social work disposals available to the courts and ensure that they are managed and supervised in such a manner that they have the confidence of courts, the police and the public at large;

- to ensure that the social work disposals are provided to the courts or other agencies in such a way that the full range of disposals is available when required so that the most appropriate one can be used, particularly with the persistent offender;

- to give priority to the development of community based social work disposals and other services to young adult offenders;

- to help offenders tackle their offending behaviour, assist them to live socially responsible lives within the law and, whenever appropriate, further their social integration through the involvement and support of their families, friends and other resources in the community.

The operation of community service by offenders in Scotland has previously been the subject of detailed research (McIvor, 1992). The present study examines the process and outcomes of probation supervision following the introduction of 100 per cent funding and National Standards.

PROBATION IN SCOTLAND

A separate probation service ceased to exist in Scotland in 1969 when its functions were absorbed into the newly created generic social work departments. Over subsequent years, however, the priority accorded to social work with offenders became eroded by the more pressing requirements of child protection work and other statutory responsibilities. This resulted in the gradual loss of confidence in probation supervision by the courts, in some parts of Scotland at least, prompting one sheriff to define probation as 'the sick man of the criminal justice system'.

The introduction of 100 per cent funding and National Standards was, therefore, viewed as crucial to restoring the confidence of the judiciary in community based social work disposals[3] and, as a consequence, diverting increasing numbers of offenders from unnecessary custodial sentences.

In Scotland courts can make a probation order for any period between six months and three years following receipt of a social enquiry report. The court can impose additional requirements (such as undertaking unpaid work, paying compensation to the victim or attendance at in intensive programme focused on tackling offending behaviour) in addition to the general requirements of the standard order, namely, that the offender is of good behaviour, complies with the directions of the supervising officer and notifies the supervisor of any change of address or employment.

Probation is defined by the Social Work Services Group of the Scottish Office as 'a means of supervising offenders in the community through a combination of control and help'. Probation 'places obligations on offenders, helps them to face their social responsibilities, and provides assistance with problems and issues associated with their offending behaviour.' Ultimately, probation 'aims to prevent or reduce further offending' (SWSG, 1993, para. 3.1).

The National Standards for probation supervision (SWSG, 1991, para. 13) identify two categories of offender to be afforded greatest priority:

- those whose current offending behaviour places them at risk of custody, who have significant underlying problems and who seem likely to re-offend, particularly young adult offenders; and

- repeat offenders with significant underlying problems whose offending history places them at risk of custody, even if the offence is trivial.

When recommending probation to the courts, the author of the Social Enquiry Report (SER) is required to develop an action plan in conjunction with the offender. According to the National Standards (SWSG, 1991, para. 20) the action plan should:

> "...set out what will be done in the course of the order to address problems and issues associated with offending behaviour with the aim of reducing the risk of re-offending. Depending on the circumstances,

---

[3] As McIvor (1995) has, however, suggested, 100 % funding for community service was necessary to prevent it becoming a victim of its own success. In some areas the court's demand for orders exceeded the availability of places in the local scheme. Some schemes responded by imposing a temporary closure on new referrals while in other orders were 'stacked' with consequent delays in the allocation of offenders to work placements and the commencement of orders. Both measures had the potential to undermine the credibility of community service with the courts. Existing funding arrangements prevented the expansion of schemes to meet the existing demand for community service by sentencers.

the plan may identify ways of tackling behavioural difficulties, personal and family problems, and may identify resources which will be used to assist the social re-integration of the offender with particular reference to such areas as education, employment and employment training, accommodation, and financial management/support."

Additional requirements may be recommended to reinforce aspects of the action plan outlined in the SER; to ensure that an element of reparation to the victim or the community is incorporated in the order; to reflect the court's concern about the seriousness of the current offence or offending history and the ensuing need for a more specific plan of action within a tighter framework of control as a means of continuing to deal with the offender in the community; or to provide the court with options which will enable its disposal of the case to reflect a balance between the interests of the offender and the interests of the victim and the wider community (SWSG, 1991, para. 24).

In the event of non-compliance with the requirements of the order or in the event of a probationer being convicted of a further offence committed whilst subject to probation supervision, the supervising social worker is required to initiate breach proceedings and return the offender to court. Where a breach is proved the court may fine the offender and allow the order to continue, vary the order (for example by attaching additional requirements) or terminate the order and sentence the offender for the original offence. Where an offender is returned to court following a conviction for a further offence the court may terminate the order and sentence for the original offence.

The supervising social worker may also apply to the court for the early discharge of an order on the grounds of good progress having been made if the probationer has not re-offended during the currency of the order, has successfully completed the tasks associated with the action plan and when no further work on issues associated with offending behaviour is believed to be necessary. In this regard the National Standards recognise that "while predicting the risk of future offending is difficult, supervisors may also wish to comment on changes in the offender's behaviour or social circumstances which would appear to render this less likely" (SWSG, 1991, para. 68).

The National Standards, in setting benchmarks against which the service can be tested and performance assessed, provide a framework for the supervision of offenders in respect of whom probation orders have been made by the court. The National Standards provide guidance on the purposes, objectives and priorities of probation orders; the social worker's role at the different stages of supervision, including the frequency of contact and requirements for formal reviews; and the steps to be taken in the event of non-compliance and in the transfer of orders to and from other jurisdictions within Scotland and in England and Wales.

The present research, in examining the process and outcomes of probation supervision in Scotland, seeks to describe the characteristics of probationers; to document the services offered by supervising social workers and the framework within which they are provided; and to examine the effectiveness of probation supervision in meeting probationers' needs and reducing the risk of further offending behaviour. More specifically, it aims to:

- identify the relationship between objectives and tasks outlined in action plans and the characteristics of individual offenders;

- examine how action plans are translated into practice, including the services and resources provided and the frequency and nature of contact between the offender, social worker and, where applicable, other agencies involved in the provision of probation services;

- consider the impact of strategic and organisational issues on the development and delivery of services to probationers;

- examine the conclusions and recommendations of reviews to assess social workers' views on the progress of individual offenders and to examine follow-up action which is taken, including applications for early discharge;

- examine the circumstances under which social workers will consider an order to have been breached, identify reasons for breach of an order and action taken by supervising officers and/or fiscals to enforce the order;

- examine the views of probationers, social workers and other agencies involved in the provision of probation services on their experiences of probation supervision, including the effectiveness of supervision at tackling behaviour associated with offending, addressing any underlying problems the offender may have and furthering the social integration of the offender into the community;

- examine the impact of probation supervision on offenders' attitudes towards their offending behaviour, on their re-offending in the short term (during their period of supervision) and on other behaviour associated with offending.

METHODOLOGY

In three of the study authorities - Bruce, Scott and Wallace - the research focused upon probation cases held by two social work teams. In the fourth area - Burns - the focus was upon the work of a single team.

In Burns social work services to the criminal justice were delivered by specialist teams. Specialist arrangements existed to middle management level for the strategic and operational management of criminal justice services, with this area of work being located at senior management level within the adult assessment section of the department, which also included community care. In Bruce criminal justice social work services were delivered by specialist teams with generic management arrangements above the level of team manager. Operational management and strategic planning and co-ordination functions had been separated and responsibility for the latter was centralised. In Scott services were delivered by practitioners in split posts, each of whom devoted a percentage of their time to offender services and the remainder to generic social work tasks. Above the level of senior social worker, generic management arrangements prevailed. Planning and co-ordination functions were, however, devolved to a specialist co-ordinator at the local level. The greatest degree of specialisation was found in Wallace, which had introduced specialist arrangements for service delivery and management to senior management level. Social workers in Scott and Wallace provided services to urban areas. Burns consisted of a small urban centre and outlying rural areas while Bruce was predominantly rural in character.

The overall study sample consisted of all probation orders which were terminated in each of the participating teams between 1 July 1994 and 30 April 1995. For a more detailed analysis of the process and outcomes of probation supervision, however, the research focused only upon those probation orders imposed by the sheriff court in each study area. In other words, orders imposed by district or high courts or orders imposed by sheriff courts outwith the study area were excluded from more detailed analysis. In Scott and Wallace, which covered more densely populated areas with a higher throughput of probation orders, an attempt was made to concentrate upon those probation cases accorded higher priority by the National Standards, that is, those in which the probationer might otherwise, had a probation order not been imposed, have been at risk of attracting a custodial sentence. The study of the probation process and outcomes therefore excluded probation orders imposed in these areas upon offenders who had no convictions in the previous three years and who had been convicted of an offence carrying a gravity rating of less than three[4].

Supervising social workers in each of the four research areas identified cases for inclusion in the study and sought the probationer's agreement a) to allow the researchers access to his/her social work file and b) to being interviewed about their experiences of probation. Such agreement was sought towards the end of the period of probation supervision, whether terminated as a consequence of successful completion, early discharge or breach.

The participating social work departments chose to adopt different approaches to recruit probationers into the sample. In Bruce and Scott, consent forms were issued in person by the supervising social worker at the last point of contact with the probationer. In Wallace, covering letters and consent forms were sent to probationers shortly after case closure. An "opt-out" policy was adopted such that probationers who did not actively withhold their consent were assumed de facto to have agreed to participate in the research. In Burns, some probationers were issued with consent forms in person by their social workers. Delays in implementing the consent forms, however, meant that most probationers were sent consent forms by post. Burns and Bruce insisted upon an 'opt-in' policy with respect to research access such that probationers could only be assumed to have consented to the researchers having access to their files if they explicitly indicated this to be the case. As a result, and as a consequence of the delay in the implementation of consent forms, the sample size in Burns was significantly smaller than in the other three areas to the extent that less reliable conclusions could be drawn about the process or effectiveness of probation supervision in that area.

The fieldwork for the research was completed between August 1994 and June 1995. The researchers visited each of the research sites on a regular basis to extract information from the case files of all probationers who had agreed to participate in the study. Information about the characteristics of probationers, their probation orders and the outcomes of orders was gathered from case files on pre-coded forms. Details of the information collected are presented in Annex I. Additional information was collected in respect of cases which involved a more detailed analysis of the process and outcomes of probation supervision. This information is presented in Annex II. The accuracy of information about the process of probation, being derived from social work case files, was dependent upon the comprehensive and accurate recording of that process in files.

After the relevant information had been extracted from case files the social worker responsible for the case was issued a questionnaire to be completed in respect of the probationer. Questionnaires were distributed only in

---

4 The gravity rating employed by Creamer et al (1993) in the calculation of a risk of custody score was employed. This assigns offences a gravity rating of one to five, with the least serious offences being assigned a gravity rating of one and the most serious a gravity rating of five. (Creamer, A., Ennis, E. and Williams, B. (1993). *The Dunscore: a method for predicting risk of custody within the Scottish context and its use in social enquiry practice.* Dundee: Department of Social Work, University of Dundee.

respect of cases which had been identified for more detailed study. The questionnaire, which included a series of fixed choice and open-ended questions, sought to elicit social workers' perceptions of the effectiveness of probation supervision in individual cases. Details of the information sought from social workers' questionnaires are presented in Annex III.

At the same time, probationers whose case files had been examined in some depth were, unless they had explicitly expressed their unwillingness to be interviewed, contacted by letter to arrange an interview in their home. The purpose of the interviews was to explore probationers' experiences and perceptions of probation supervision. The issues addressed in the interviews, which lasted, on average, between one and one and a half hours and were semi-structured, are presented in Annex IV.

The total sample consisted of 155 probation orders, 112 of which were subjected to a detailed analysis of the process and outcomes of supervision. Completed social workers' questionnaires were returned in respect of 96 of the smaller sample of 112 probationers and 65 probationers from this smaller sample were interviewed. Thirty-seven other probationers agreed to be interviewed but failed to keep appointments with the researcher. Ten others had agreed to the researchers having access to their files but were unwilling to be interviewed, usually because they did not want to discuss their offences or wished, more generally, to put their offences and experience of the criminal justice system behind them.

Similar reasons were advanced by social workers for the refusal on the part of 11 probationers to agree to research access to their files and participation in the study. On the basis of brief anonymised information provided by social workers on pre-coded forms in the event of their probationer's refusal (which included gender, age, length of order, nature of any additional requirements, main offence, criminal history, and reason for termination of the order) there was no evidence that probationers who refused access differed in any marked respect from those who allowed the researchers access to their files. Nor did probationers who refused to be interviewed differ in any obvious respect from the total sample of which they were a part. Finally, the cases on which social workers completed questionnaires appeared to be largely similar to the sample as a whole. Therefore unless social workers exercised some discretion in respect of the cases identified for inclusion on the study, it can be assumed that the findings presented in this report are, in general, representative of probation practice in the participating study areas.

Interviews were conducted with social work managers, with social workers and with independent sector services providers in each of the four areas in the context of the other studies within the present research programme. Where relevant, information derived from these interviews has been drawn upon in the present report to address the research questions previously outlined in this chapter.

CHAPTER TWO

OFFENDERS MADE SUBJECT TO PROBATION SUPERVISION

INTRODUCTION

The present chapter describes the characteristics of 155 offenders sentenced to probation across the four study areas: five in Burns, 26 in Bruce, 50 in Scott and 74 in Wallace. In view of the small numbers in Burns, these cases have been included in the overall analysis but, while reference will be made to them where relevant, have been excluded from comparisons of samples across areas. The cases described in this chapter are all of those in respect of which research access was granted. Subsequent chapters focus upon a smaller sub-sample of these cases which were examined in greater detail.

THE CHARACTERISTICS OF ORDERS

The majority of probation orders (85 per cent) were imposed by the sheriff court under summary proceedings. Of the remainder, eight were imposed by district courts, six by sheriff courts under solemn proceedings, and four by the high and appeal courts. One order was made by the stipendiary magistrates' court and four by courts outwith Scotland. As Table 2.1 indicates, 42 per cent of probationers had been ordained to appear for sentence and a similar percentage (41 per cent) had been bailed. Seventeen per cent of probationers had been remanded in custody. In four cases (three per cent) the form of continuation was unknown. Offenders in Bruce were most likely to have been ordained to appear for sentence and least likely to have been remanded in custody or bailed. Offenders in Scott were more likely to have been remanded in custody prior to sentence.

Table 2.1: Form of continuation by area

	Bruce	Scott	Wallace	Total[5]
Ordained	18 (69%)	17 (34%)	26 (37%)	63 (42%)
Bailed	6 (23%)	21 (42%)	34 (49%)	62 (41%)
Remanded in custody	2 (8%)	12 (24%)	10 (14%)	26 (17%)
Total	26	50	70	151[6]

The average length of order imposed was 14.6 months. While Burns had the shortest average length of order at 8.4 months, there were no significant differences in this respect between the other three areas. The average length of order was 14.8 months in Bruce, 14.5 months in Scott and 15.0 months in Wallace. Fifty-nine per cent of probation orders (92) were for 12 months and only two were for periods in excess of 24 months. As Table 2.2 indicates, a slightly higher proportion of orders in Bruce were for 12 months or less.

Table 2.2: Length of order by area

	Bruce	Scott	Wallace	Total[7]
12 months or less	21 (81%)	33 (66%)	48 (64%)	107 (69%)
More than 12 months	5 (19%)	17 (34%)	26 (36%)	48 (30%)
Total	26	50	74	155

The length of order imposed appeared to be unrelated to a number of sentencing variables such as previous convictions and previous custodial sentences. Orders imposed on young offenders did not differ from those imposed on adults and men, and women were given probation orders of similar lengths. The only factor which appeared to be related to the length of probation order was the gravity rating[8] of the main offence: 25 per cent of probationers sentenced for an offence carrying a gravity rating of less than three were given orders of 18

---

[5] Includes the five cases in Burns.
[6] Data missing in four cases.
[7] Includes the five cases in Burns.
[8] See the footnote on page 4 for an explanation of the gravity rating.

months or more compared with 35 per cent of those sentenced for an offence with a gravity rating of three or more.

Just over half the orders made (84 orders or 54 per cent) carried no additional requirements. The majority of additional requirements related to the completion by the offender of unpaid work (22 orders) or attendance at an intensive probation programme (19 orders). Other requirements less frequently attached included alcohol counselling (8 orders), payment of compensation (7 orders), psychiatric treatment (6 orders), drug counselling (5 orders) and attendance at other special programmes (4 orders). As Table 2.3 shows, there was relatively little difference across areas in respect of the percentage of probation orders to which additional requirements were attached.

Table 2.3: Type of order by area

	Bruce	Scott	Wallace	Total[9]
Probation	12 (46%)	28 (56%)	40 (54%)	85 (54%)
Probation and other requirements	14 (54%)	22 (44%)	34 (46%)	70 (46%)
Total	26	50	74	155

In Burns one order carried a requirement to perform community service and this also formed the basis of the majority of additional requirements (10) in Bruce. Most additional requirements in Scott related to community service (9) or attendance at an intensive probation programme (7). Only two orders in Wallace contained a requirement to undertake community service (this option having only recently become available in that area). Whilst 11 probationers in Wallace were required to attend an intensive probation programme, probationers in this area were also more likely than those in the other areas to have a range of other conditions attached. The nature of additional requirements across the research sites tended to reflect the availability of services. Bruce, for instance, was the only area not to have a designated intensive probation project (though intensive groupwork was undertaken by area team social workers when resources permitted) hence the relatively high use of community service as a requirement of probation.

Probationers whose orders contained additional requirements had, on average, more convictions in the three years prior to sentence (6.1 compared with 3.8) and had served, on average, more custodial sentences during the same period (1.4 compared with 0.6). First or early offenders with fewer than three previous convictions were less likely than probationers with six or more previous convictions to have additional requirements attached to their probation orders (41 per cent compared with 51 per cent). Additional requirements were more likely to be attached to orders imposed on offenders who were sentenced for offences involving dishonesty (50 per cent compared with 40 per cent for other types of offences) and on offenders who had previously been sentenced to a community based social work disposal (58 per cent compared with 34 per cent). Young offenders were more likely to be given a probation order with additional requirements than were adults (53 per cent compared with 39 per cent) and men were more likely than women to have received a probation order with a condition attached (52 per cent compared with 18 per cent).

THE CHARACTERISTICS OF PROBATIONERS

Across the sample as a whole 82 per cent of probationers (127) were male and 18 per cent (28) were female. One probationer in Burns was a woman. The highest proportion of women probationers was found in Bruce, where women made up 31 per cent of the sample compared with 14 per cent in Scott and 16 per cent in Wallace.

Just under half the sample (75 probationers or 48 per cent) were between 16 and 20 years of age. Just over half the male probationers (52 per cent) were under 21 years of age compared with around a third of females (32 per cent). Four of the five probationers in Burns were 21 years of age or older. The average age of women probationers was higher than the average age of males (27.0 years compared with 23.0 years). The average ages of probationers did not differ significantly across the other three areas (being 24.8 years, 23.3 years and 23.5 years in Bruce, Scott and Wallace respectively) though there was a slightly lower proportion of young offenders in Bruce compared with the other two areas (42 per cent compared with 50 and 51 per cent).

Seventy-two per cent of probationers (111) were single when their probation order was imposed, 19 per cent (30) were married or co-habiting and nine per cent were widowed, separated or divorced. Twenty per cent of the sample (31 probationers) had dependent children living with them and 14 per cent had dependent children living elsewhere. Women probationers were less likely than men to be single (50 per cent compared

---

9 Includes the five cases in Burns.

with 76 per cent) and were more likely to be married or co-habiting (36 per cent compared with 16 per cent). Women were, in addition, more likely than men to have children living in the same household (54 per cent compared with 13 per cent)

Across the sample as a whole, 83 per cent of probationers were unemployed at the point of sentence. Four of the five probationers in Burns were unemployed. The percentages unemployed in Bruce, Scott and Wallace were 77 per cent, 80 per cent and 86 per cent respectively. Seventy-five per cent of the sample were living either in the parental home (43 per cent) or in their own or shared tenancy (32 per cent) when made subject to probation.

The Offence

Fifty-seven per cent of probationers had received their orders for main offences involving dishonesty (Table 2.4). Two of the five probationers in Burns had received probation for offences involving dishonesty. In Bruce 10 probationers (38 per cent) were given probation for offences of this type compared with 30 (60 per cent) in Scott and 46 (62 per cent) in Wallace.

Table 2.4: Nature of main offence

	Number of cases	Percentage of cases
Dishonesty	88	57
Common assault/breach of the peace	30	19
Road traffic	12	8
Non-sexual crimes of violence	11	7
Drugs	9	6
Criminal damage	2	1
Wasting police time	2	1
Sexual	1	<1
Total	155	100

Young offenders were more likely than adults to have received probation for offences involving dishonesty (68 per cent compared with 46 per cent). Women were just as likely as men to have been placed on probation for offences of this type (57 per cent of men and 57 per cent of women). Within this broader category, however, males were more likely to have been convicted of housebreakings and car thefts while women were more likely to have been sentenced for theft or fraud. Offenders sentenced to probation for offences involving dishonesty had slightly more previous convictions (9.1 compared with 6.8) and had served, on average, more previous custodial sentences (2.3 compared with 0.7) than offenders who received probation orders for other types of offences. Persistent offenders (those with 6 or more previous convictions) were more likely than first or early offenders (with fewer than three previous convictions) to have received probation for offences involving dishonesty (66 per cent compared with 56 per cent).

Thirty-three per cent of probationers received probation for a single offence. Fifty per cent had been convicted of between two and four offences while 17 per cent were sentenced for five or more offences. Offenders in Wallace were, on average, sentenced for slightly more offences than were probationers in Bruce and Scott (3.4 offences compared with 2.7 and 2.7 respectively). Women were given probation for slightly fewer offences than men (2.2 compared with 3.1) while young offenders were sentenced for a higher average number of offences than adults (3.7 compared with 2.3). First or early offenders were sentenced for fewer offences on average than were persistent offenders (2.3 compared with 3.3).

Forty-one per cent of probationers were given probation for a main offence carrying a gravity rating of one or two. Fifty-three per cent of the main offences resulting in the imposition of a probation order carried a gravity rating of three. Only ten probationers (6 per cent) were sentenced for an offence with a gravity rating of four or five. The average gravity ratings of main offences in Bruce, Scott and Wallace were similar at 2.3, 2.3 and 2.5 respectively. The average gravity ratings of offences committed by men and women were likewise similar at 2.4 and 2.5 and young offenders were sentenced for offences which carried gravity ratings similar to those for which adults were convicted (2.5 compared with 2.3). The average gravity rating of the main offences in respect of which probationers were sentenced was slightly higher for first or early offenders than for persistent offenders (2.6 compared with 2.3): 30 per cent of first or early offenders were given probation for a main offence carrying a gravity rating of less than three compared with 42 per cent of persistent offenders. This would suggest that in the case of persistent offenders the seriousness of previous criminal history rather than the seriousness of the current offence was more likely to be a factor influencing sentencing decisions.

Previous Convictions

Across the whole sample, probationers had, on average, 8.1 previous convictions in total and 4.8 in the previous three years. They had served an average of 3.9 custodial sentences in total and 2.3 in the previous three years. Probationers in Wallace had the highest average number of previous convictions both in total and in the previous three years while probationers in Bruce had the fewest. Probationers in Wallace had, in addition, served more custodial sentences, on average, than probationers in the other two areas (Table 2.5).

Table 2.5: Previous convictions and custodial sentences by area

	Bruce (n=26)	Scott (n=50)	Wallace (n=74)
Previous convictions	3.8	7.6	10.0
In last 3 years	2.0	4.4	6.2
Previous custodial sentences	0.3	1.4	2.3
In last 3 years	0.2	0.9	1.3

Fourteen per cent of probationers had no previous convictions (19 per cent, 14 per cent and 12 percent in Bruce, Scott and Wallace respectively). Fifty-one per cent of the sample, however, had six or more previous convictions when given their probation orders. Probationers in Wallace were more likely to have six or more previous convictions (60 per cent) than probationers in Scott (48 per cent) and Bruce (27 per cent). Women had, on average, fewer previous convictions than men (4.6 compared with 8.9).

Thirty per cent of the sample had served at least one previous custodial sentence and 14 per cent had been imprisoned or detained on at least five occasions. Probationers in Bruce were less likely than those in Scott and Wallace to have served a previous custodial sentence (11 per cent compared with 40 per cent and 31 per cent). Women were more likely than men to be first offenders (33 per cent compared with 7 per cent) and were less likely to have previous experience of custody (6 per cent compared with 36 per cent).

Just over half the probationers (51 per cent) had previous experience of community based social work disposals. Thirty-two percent had been on probation in the past and 34 per cent had previously been sentenced to a community service order. Sixteen per cent of the sample had previous experience of both probation and community service. Four offenders in Burns had no previous experience of social work disposals and one had served a community service order.

As Table 2.6 indicates, probationers in Bruce were least likely to have previously been given a community based social work disposal by the courts.

Table 2.6: Previous community based social work disposals by area[10]

	Bruce (n=26)	Scott (n=50)	Wallace[11] (n=73)
None	17 (65%)	21 (42%)	34 (47%)
Probation	6 (23%)	19 (38%)	25 (34%)

Forty-five per cent of probationers were known to have been subject to supervision through the children's hearing system. Thirty-six (23 per cent) had been the subject of a residential supervision requirement, 30 (19 per cent) had been on home supervision orders and three had been subject to voluntary supervision by the social work department. The relevant data were unavailable in two cases. There were no significant differences

---

[10] Column totals exceed the total sample size in Scott and Wallace since some offenders had previously been sentenced to both community service and probation.
[11] Data missing in one case.

in the proportions of probationers who had been subject to different forms of supervision across the different areas though probationers in Wallace were slightly more likely to have been subject to residential requirements (29 per cent of probationers in this area).

Risk of Custody

When completing social enquiry report core data returns for the Scottish Office, social workers are asked to record whether or not they consider custody to have been a likely option in each case. Social workers' assessments of the likelihood of custody could be located for 121[12] probationers in the sample. In 38 per cent of cases the social worker believed that custody had been a likely option for the probationer. In a similar proportion of cases (40 per cent) custody was considered unlikely. In 22 per cent of cases the social worker did not know if custody was a likely option or not. The relevant data are summarised by area in Table 2.7.

Table 2.7: Social workers' assessments of custody risk

	Bruce	Scott	Wallace	Total
Custody likely	4 (18%)	11 (28%)	31 (52%)	46 (38%)
Custody not likely	13 (59%)	12 (31%)	23 (38%)	48 (40%)
Don't know	5 (23%)	16 (41%)	6 (10%)	27 (22%)
Total	22	39	60	121

Probationers in Bruce were least likely to be considered at risk of custody while those in Wallace were most likely to be thought at risk of attracting a custodial sentence. Taking into account only those cases in which social workers expressed a clear opinion, it is found that 24 per cent of probationers in Bruce (4 out of 17) were thought to be at risk of custody compared with 48 per cent in Scott (11 out of 23) and 57 per cent (31 out of 54) in Wallace. This pattern of findings is consistent with the earlier observation that offenders in Wallace had the most serious criminal histories and those in Bruce the fewest previous convictions, custodial sentences and social work disposals.

Probationers whose orders contained additional requirements were more likely than those whose orders did not to be considered at risk of custody (51 per cent compared with 28 per cent). Perceived custody risk also differed according to the characteristics of the probationers.

Thus young offenders were more often considered at risk of custody than adults (42 per cent compared with 34 per cent); men were more likely to be thought at risk of custody than women (42 per cent compared with 23 per cent); persistent offenders were more likely to be viewed as being at risk of custody than were first or early offenders (52 per cent compared with 24 per cent); and probationers who had been given their orders for offences involving dishonesty were more often thought to be at risk of custody (43 per cent) than those whose orders had been imposed in respect of offences involving breaches of public order or violence (32 per cent) or other miscellaneous offences (33 per cent).

PRE-SENTENCE ASSESSMENTS AND RECOMMENDATIONS

Social and Personal Problems

The types of social and personal problems experienced by this sample of probationers prior to being placed on probation are summarised in Table 2.8.

Offenders in the different areas were equally likely to have family problems and to be involved in the misuse of drugs. The incidence of alcohol related problems was highest in Scott and lowest in Bruce, the incidence of mental health problems was highest in Bruce and lowest in Wallace, while persistent offending was most often identified as an issue in Wallace and accommodation was more often said to be a problem in Scott.

Male and female probationers were equally likely to have been identified as experiencing family problems and to be involved in the misuse of drugs. Men were twice as likely as women to have problems related to the abuse of alcohol while women were more likely to be identified as experiencing mental health problems, bereavement or loss. None of the women were described as persistent offenders or said to be entrenched in an offending peer group.

---

[12] This information was available in respect of only one case in Burns which has been excluded from the analysis.

Table 2.8: Problems identified in SERs

	Number of cases (n=155)	Percentage of cases
Family relationships/problems	59	38
Drug abuse	49	32
Alcohol abuse	40	26
Mental health[13]	19	12
Medical	18	12
Educational[14]	18	12
Child care history	13	8
Immaturity/vulnerability[15]	13	8
Accommodation	12	8
Financial problems	12	8
Persistent offending	12	8
Bereavement/loss/grief	12	8
Long term unemployment	9	6
Low self-esteem	8	5
Aggression	8	5
Peer group	7	5
Boredom/use of leisure time	5	3
Personal relationships	3	2
Other[16]	3	2
No problems identified	8	5

Alcohol abuse was twice as likely to feature among adult offenders though the incidence of drug abuse was similar among young offenders and adults. Older offenders were more likely to have medical and mental health problems while younger offenders were more likely to be identified as having family problems and problems relating to low educational achievement.

Explanations for Offending

The explanations offered by social workers for the offences committed by the probationers are summarised in Table 2.9. In around a third of cases (34 per cent) offending was linked to alcohol abuse and in around a fifth of cases (21 per cent) offences were said to have been committed under the influence of, or to obtain money for, drugs.

Offending was most likely to be linked to alcohol abuse in Scott (50 per cent of cases compared with 28 per cent in Bruce and 30 per cent in Wallace) and less likely in Bruce than in either Scott or Wallace to have been related to drug misuse (8 per cent, 33 per cent and 24 per cent of cases respectively). Financial gain was most often advanced as an explanation for offending in Wallace (31 per cent of cases compared with 10 per cent in Bruce and 13 per cent in Scott) whilst offenders in Bruce were more likely than those in the other two areas to have their offending explained as a reaction to emotional pressures (30 per cent compared with 13 per cent in Scott and 10 per cent in Wallace). The explanations for offending most commonly provided in Bruce were emotional pressures (30 per cent), alcohol abuse (28 per cent) and peer group pressure (25 per cent). Alcohol abuse (50 per cent), drug abuse (33 per cent) and peer group pressure (24 per cent) featured most often in Scott, while financial gain (31 per cent) alcohol abuse (30 per cent) and opportunism/impulsiveness (30 per cent) predominated in Wallace.

---

[13] Includes two offenders with previous suicide attempts.
[14] Low educational achievement (10) literacy problems (4) learning difficulties (4).
[15] Immaturity (5) social isolation (5) lacking social skills (1) unable to cope on own (1) physical appearance (1).
[16] Victim of sexual abuse (2) gambling (1).

Table 2.9: Explanations for offending offered in SERs

	Number of cases (n=155)	Percentage of cases
Alcohol related	53	34
Drug related[17]	33	21
Opportunistic/impulsive[18]	32	21
Financial gain	29	19
Peer group pressure	27	17
Emotional pressure[19]	20	13
Provocation/defence	9	6
Boredom/seeking excitement	9	6
Lack of parental guidance	3	2
Other[20]	6	4
None given	9	6

Male offenders were more likely than females to be described as having offended under the influence of alcohol (40 per cent compared with 22 per cent), to have acted impulsively without considering the consequences (23 per cent compared with 18 per cent) or to have committed offences to relieve boredom (8 per cent of males but no females). Women's offences, on the other hand, were said more often than men's to have been committed for financial gain (33 per cent compared with 17 per cent) or as a consequence of emotional stress (18 per cent compared with 13 per cent). Alcohol abuse (40 per cent), drug abuse (23 per cent), opportunism/impulsiveness (23 per cent) and peer group pressure (19 per cent) were the explanations for offending most commonly offered in respect of males. Financial gain (33 per cent), alcohol abuse (22 per cent) and drug abuse (22 per cent) were most often advanced as explanations for women's offending.

Young offenders were more likely to be described as having offended impulsively (35 per cent compared with 11 per cent of adults), in response to boredom (10 per cent compared with 3 per cent) or under the influence of offending peers (31 per cent compared with 8 per cent). Adults, on the other hand, were more likely to have offended under the influence of alcohol (48 per cent compared with 25 per cent) or in response to emotional pressures (20 per cent compared with 9 per cent). Opportunism/impulsiveness (35 per cent), peer group pressure (31 per cent), drug abuse (26 per cent) and alcohol abuse (25 per cent) were most often advanced as reasons for offending by probationers under 21 years of age. Alcohol abuse (48 per cent), drug abuse (20 per cent), emotional pressure (20 per cent) and financial gain (19 per cent) were the explanations most often offered for offending by adults.

First or early offenders (that is, those with fewer than three previous convictions) were more likely than persistent offenders (those with six or more previous convictions) to have been described as offending in response to peer group pressure (23 per cent compared with 12 per cent). Persistent offenders, on the other hand, were more likely to have been assessed as offending as a consequence of alcohol abuse (46 per cent compared with 21 per cent) or drug abuse (31 per cent compared with 16 per cent). The explanations most commonly advanced in respect of first or early offenders were opportunism/impulsivenenss (28 per cent), peer group pressure (23 per cent), financial gain (23 per cent) and alcohol abuse (21 per cent). Persistent offenders were most likely to have been described as offending as a consequence of alcohol abuse (46 per cent), drug abuse (31 per cent), opportunism/impulsiveness (22 per cent) or financial gain (18 per cent).

Explanations for offending also differed according to the type of main offence. For the purpose of analysis, a comparison was made between probationers convicted of offences involving dishonesty ("dishonesty" offenders), those convicted of assaults, breaches of the peace and non-sexual crimes of violence ("conduct" offenders) and the smaller numbers of offenders convicted of a range of other offence types ("other" offenders).

Drug abuse was most likely to feature in the explanations of offending pertaining to "dishonesty" offenders (31 per cent compared with 8 per cent of "conduct" offenders and 20 per cent of "other"[21] offenders) as was

---

[17] Includes three cases of solvent abuse.

[18] Lack of self control (9) failure to consider consequences (9) opportunistic (7) violent tendencies (5) naiveté (2).

[19] Emotional stress (15) illness in family (4) marital difficulties (1).

[20] Limited budgeting skills (1) pain relief (1) low expectation of ability to stop offending (1) cry for help (1) limited intelligence (1) homelessness (1).

[21] This category includes probationers who received their orders for drug offences.

financial gain (32 per cent compared with 3 per cent of "conduct" offenders and 8 per cent of "other" offenders).

Explanations of offending offered in respect of "conduct" offenders were most likely to include reference to alcohol abuse (57 per cent compared with 30 per cent of "dishonesty" offenders and 32 per cent of "other" offenders). Offenders in this category were also more likely to have been described as offending as a consequence of emotional pressure (27 per cent compared with 10 per cent of "dishonesty" offenders and 8 per cent of "other" offenders) or through provocation or defence of self or others (19 per cent compared with 7 per cent and 12 per cent).

Financial gain (32 per cent), drug abuse (31 per cent) and alcohol abuse (30 per cent) were the explanations most often advanced in relation to "dishonesty" offenders. "Conduct" offenders were most likely to have been assessed as offending as a consequence of alcohol abuse (57 per cent), opportunism/impulsiveness (27 per cent) or emotional pressure (27 per cent). Alcohol abuse (32 per cent), drug abuse (20 per cent), opportunism/impulsiveness and peer group pressure (each 16 per cent) featured most commonly in the explanations of offending provided for the mixed group of "other" offenders.

SER Recommendations

The disposals which had been recommended by social workers in SERs are summarised in Table 2.10. The majority of probation orders made (74%) followed a recommendation for probation with or without additional requirements. Fifteen per cent of orders, however, followed a recommendation for an alternative sentence and in just over 10 per cent of cases in which a probation order was imposed, no clear recommendation had been presented to the court.

Thirty-two per cent of probation recommendations included an additional requirement. In nineteen cases the additional requirement related to attendance at an intensive probation or other special programme. Community service was recommended as an additional requirement in seven cases and alcohol counselling in a further five. Drugs counselling and psychiatric treatment were each recommended twice, while compensation and residential requirements were each recommended on one occasion.

Table 2.10: Recommendations contained in SERs

	Number of cases (n=155)	Percentage of cases
Probation	78	50
Probation with additional requirements	37	24
Deferred sentence	16	10
Community service	5	3
Fine	1	<1
Admonition	1	<1
Refer to children's hearing	1	<1
No clear recommendation	16	10

The pattern of recommendations by area is summarised in Table 2.11. All five recommendations in Burns were for probation without additional requirements. Additional requirements were least likely to be recommended in Scott while probation orders in Wallace were most likely to have followed a recommendation for probation with or without additional requirements. Almost half the probation recommendations in Bruce (47 per cent) contained additional requirements (in five cases community service) compared with 20 per cent in Scott and 37 per cent in Wallace.

The relatively high level of recommendations for probation with an additional requirement in Bruce is somewhat surprising given that, as we have seen, probationers in this area tended to have less extensive criminal histories and were less likely to be considered at risk of custody than those in the other research sites. It is not without coincidence, perhaps, that unlike their colleagues in Scott and Wallace, social workers in Bruce did not draw upon the Dunscore[22] as a mechanism for targeting community based social work disposals.

[22] A method of calculating the risk of custody facing an offender when she/he appears before the court, based on a statistical analysis of data collected in research sites across Scotland. It gives numerical weighting to those factors most significantly associated with custodial outcomes and can be adjusted to account for local court sentencing practice (Creamer et al., 1993).

Such a development was said by a social work manager to have been resisted by staff, who considered it both threatening and undermining of their professional judgement. The same manager also explained that the sheriff in Bruce was opposed to explicit targeting and, in particular, to the inclusion in SERs of references to the perceived risk of custody faced by the offender.

Table 2.11: SER recommendations by area

	Bruce	Scott	Wallace	Total
Probation	9 (35%)	27 (54%)	37 (50%)	73 (49%)
Probation with additional requirements	8 (31%)	7 (14%)	22 (30%)	37 (25%)
Other disposal	6 (23%)	9 (18%)	9 (12%)	24 (16%)
No clear recommendation	3 (12%)	7 (14%)	6 (8%)	16 (11%)
Total	26	50	74	150

Thirty-six percent of probation recommendations for males included reference to additional requirements compared with 11 per cent of those for females: only two of the probation recommendations which contained reference to additional requirements related to female probationers (one each for community service and drug counselling). Thirty-six per cent of probation recommendations for young offenders contained additional requirements compared with 28 per cent of those relating to offenders aged 21 years or older. The absence of a clear recommendation was more likely in the case of older probationers than those under 21 years of age (15 per cent compared with 5 per cent).

There was no clear relationship between the proportion of probation recommendations containing reference to additional requirements and the main offence for which probationers were being sentenced. However, first or early offenders (that is, those with fewer than three previous convictions) were less likely than persistent offenders (with six or more previous convictions) to have additional requirements included within probation recommendations (28 per cent compared with 37 per cent).

The reasons put forward by social workers when recommending probation orders to the courts are summarised in Table 2.12. They generally fell into five broader categories: to address or monitor offending behaviour; to address behaviour associated with offending; to provide help with practical problems; to provide support or help of a more general kind; and to build upon the offender's motivation to change or his/her probability of responding positively to probation. It should be noted that category percentage totals cannot be included in Table 2.12 since some probationers were included more than once within a particular category.

Explicit reference to addressing offending behaviour was less common in Bruce where it featured in 35 per cent of cases compared to 47 per cent of those in Scott and 52 per cent in Wallace. Probation was more likely to be recommended in Bruce than in Scott and Wallace to provide help with employment or education (35 per cent, 18 per cent and 22 per cent of cases respectively) or with housing (24 per cent, 3 per cent and 14 per cent), to address relationship problems (24 per cent, 9 per cent and 8 per cent) or to address violence or aggression (24 per cent, 0 per cent and 7 per cent). Drug abuse more often featured as a reason for recommending probation in Scott (26 per cent) than in Bruce (18 per cent) or Wallace (20 per cent). Probation was recommended as a means of monitoring offenders' behaviour in 18 per cent of cases in Scott but only 7 per cent in Wallace and none in Bruce. Providing help with financial problems was more often advanced as a reason for recommending probation in Wallace (14 per cent) than in Scott (9 per cent) or Bruce (6 per cent).

Women were less likely to be recommended for probation as a means of addressing offending behaviour (39 per cent compared with 51 per cent of men) or alcohol abuse (11 per cent compared with 34 per cent) and probation was more likely to be recommended for women than for men as a vehicle for accessing support of a general kind (28 per cent compared with 9 per cent). The main reasons for recommending probation for male offenders were as a means of addressing offending (51 per cent), addressing alcohol abuse (34 per cent), providing help with employment or education (23 per cent) and addressing drug use (22 per cent). Addressing offending behaviour (39 per cent), providing general support (28 per cent) and addressing drug use (22 per cent) were the reasons most often advanced in support of probation recommendations for women.

Young offenders were less often recommended for probation as a means of addressing problematic drug (16 per cent compared with 28 per cent) or alcohol (21 per cent compared with 41 per cent) use, while providing help with employment was more often advanced in support of probation for young offenders than for adults (28 per cent compared with 15 per cent). Early or first offenders were more likely than persistent offenders to have

probation recommended as a means of addressing relationship problems (19 per cent compared with 10 per cent) or financial problems (16 per cent compared with 7 per cent). Persistent offenders were more likely than first or early offenders to be recommended for probation to address offending behaviour (60 per cent compared with 41 per cent), to address drug use (25 per cent compared with 16 per cent), to be provided with general support (18 compared with 6 per cent) or to be provided with help in relation to housing (18 per cent compared with 6 per cent).

Table 2.12: Reasons for recommending probation

	Number of cases (n=115)	Percentage of cases
Addressing/monitoring offending behaviour		
To address offending behaviour	61	53
To monitor behaviour	10	9
Addressing behaviour associated with offending		
To address alcohol abuse	35	30
To address drug abuse	26	23
To address violence/aggression	12	10
To address peer group pressure	8	7
Providing help with practical problems		
Help with employment/education	27	24
Help with accommodation	13	11
Help with financial problems	12	10
To develop practical skills[23]	6	5
To address use of leisure time	5	4
Providing general help or support		
General support and advice	21	18
Develop personal/social skills[24]	20	17
Help with relationship problems	18	16
To provide emotional support[25]	15	13
To provide continuity/focus/purpose	10	9
Building on offender's motivation or likely response to probation		
Offender motivated to make use of probation	12	9
Offender may benefit from probation	10	9
Has benefited from probation in the past	5	4
Other[26]	04	3

Reasons for recommending probation also varied according to the type of main offence. Addressing offending featured more often among "dishonesty" offenders than among "conduct" and "other" offenders (59 per cent compared with 38 per cent and 35 per cent respectively). Addressing alcohol use was most often referred to in the case of "conduct" offenders (62 per cent compared with 15 per cent of "dishonesty" offenders and 35 per cent of "other" offenders) as was addressing aggression or violence (34 per cent compared with 3 per cent of "dishonesty" offenders and no "other" offenders). Drug use was less often advanced as a reason for recommending probation in the case of "conduct" offenders than those convicted of "dishonesty" or "other" offences (14 per cent compared with 23 per cent and 30 per cent).

THE OUTCOMES OF ORDERS

The outcomes of probation orders and the processes associated with differential outcomes will be examined in some detail in the following chapter. Here, however, the focus is primarily upon factors associated with the increased likelihood of an order being breached.

A total of 38 orders (25 per cent of the sample) were revoked as a consequence of breach, 91 (59 per cent) were completed successfully and 21 (14 per cent) were discharged early. One offender died prior to completion of his order and four other orders were transferred to another area prior to completion. Taking into account

---

[23] Child care (3) literacy (3).
[24] Self esteem (8) social skills (6) deal with problems more effectively (5) impulsiveness (1).
[25] Bereavement counselling (8) rape counselling (2) counselling regarding illness (1) depression (1) emotional problems (1) anxiety (1) vulnerability (1).
[26] Support for family (1) unlikely to re-offend (1) no previous social work disposal (1) could not cope with prison (1).

only those 150 orders breached or completed (in full or through early discharge), a range of differences emerged between the two groups of probationers.

As Table 2.13 illustrates, women were less likely than men to be breached and were more likely to have their probation orders discharged early. The higher incidence of early discharge cannot be accounted for by the fact that women were sentenced to longer probation orders. Instead, it is more likely to reflect the perception that women, who had shorter criminal histories, were less likely, once their immediate problems had been addressed, to present a risk of continued offending.

Table 2.13: Outcome of orders and gender

	Male	Female	Total
Early discharge	14 (11%)	7 (26%)	21 (14%)
Completion	73 (59%)	18 (67%)	91 (61%)
Breach	36 (29%)	2 (7%)	38 (25%)

There was an association between the outcome of orders and age: the average age of probationers who were breached was 20.7 years compared with 26.5 years for early discharges and 24.5 years for offenders who completed their orders in full. As Table 2.14 indicates, young offenders were three times as likely as adults to be breached while adults were almost twice as likely as young offenders to have their probation orders discharged early.

Table 2.14: Outcome of orders and age

	16-20 years	21 years and over	Total
Early discharge	7 (10%)	14 (18%)	21 (14%)
Completion	38 (52%)	53 (69%)	91 (61%)
Breach	28 (38%)	10 (13%)	38 (25%)
Total	73	77	150

A clear relationship was found between criminal history and the likelihood of breach. Probationers who were breached had an average of 11.5 previous convictions and had served, on average, 3.1 previous custodial sentences. This compares with an average of 6.7 previous convictions and 1.0 previous custodial sentences among probationers whose orders were successfully completed in full or as a consequence of early discharge. The greatest risk of breach was found amongst offenders with 11 or more previous convictions, 38 per cent of whom were breached compared to 25 per cent of those with 10 or fewer convictions and 5 per cent of those with none. Likewise, probationers who had previously served five or more custodial sentences were more likely to be breached (53 per cent) than those who had served between one and four sentences of detention or imprisonment (27 per cent of whom were breached) or who had served none (20 per cent).

Other factors found to be associated with an increased risk of breach were the type of offence for which offenders received their probation order and the gravity rating of the main offence. Thus offenders who received probation for offences involving dishonesty were more likely than those sentenced for other offences to be breached (34 per cent compared with 14 per cent). Probationers whose main offence carried a gravity rating of three or more were more likely to be breached than those whose main offence had a gravity rating of one or two (35 per cent compared with 11 per cent). However, the majority of offences carrying a higher gravity rating involved dishonesty and offenders who were given probation orders for offences involving dishonesty tended to be younger and to have more previous convictions and previous custodial sentences than those who received probation for other types of offences. It would appear, therefore, that criminal history and age were more powerful determinants of the risk of breach than the type of offence or gravity rating per se.

Previous criminal history is, of course, a critical factor in determining risk of custody. Cases in which social workers believed that the probationer had been at risk of attracting a custodial sentence when made subject to probation were three times as likely to be breached as those in which custody was considered unlikely (47 per cent compared with 15 per cent).

There was no indication that longer probation orders were more likely to be breached than shorter orders. The average length of breached orders was 15.0 months compared with 13.5 months for orders which were completed in full. Similarly, the breach rate for orders up to 12 months in length was 25 per cent compared with 27 per cent for those of 18 months or more. Longer orders were, however, more likely to be discharged early than shorter orders: only 9 per cent of orders up to and including 12 months were discharged early compared with 27 per cent of orders of 18 months or more.

Probation orders with additional requirements were more likely to be breached than orders without additional requirements attached (33 per cent compared with 19 per cent). This again, however, may to a greater extent reflect the differing criminal histories or ages of probationers given different types of orders rather than the presence of additional requirements per se.

The breach rate varied across the research sites. None of the orders in Burns were terminated through breach. As Table 2.15 shows, the breach rate was highest in Wallace, while probationers in Bruce were most likely to have their probation orders discharged early. Again it is likely that the pattern of outcomes reflects the characteristics of offenders made subject to probation across the three areas.

Table 2.15: Outcome of orders by area

	Bruce	Scott	Wallace	Total
Early discharge	8 (31%)	6 (12%)	7 (10%)	21 (14%)
Completion	17 (65%)	33 (69%)	36 (51%)	91 (61%)
Breach	1 (4%)	9 (19%)	28 (39%)	38 (25%)
Total	26	48	71	150

Social Circumstances of Probationers

Turning finally to the social circumstances of probationers on termination of their orders, there was some evidence that in some cases these had improved over the course of probation.

As Tables 2.16 and 2.17 indicate, offenders were more likely to be employed at the end of their probation order than at the start and they were more likely to have a tenancy. This is consistent with the views of offenders and supervising social workers in Chapters Four and Five that some progress had been made in a number of cases with respect to the securing of employment and accommodation.

Table 2.16: Employment status at start and end of order

	Start of order	End of order
Unemployed	128 (83%)	115 (74%)
Employed	10 (6%)	32 (21%)
Not seeking work	9 (6%)	5 (3%)
Government training scheme	7 (5%)	3 (2%)
Full-time education	1 (<1%)	-
Total	155	155

Table 2.17: Accommodation at start and end of order

	Start of order	End of order
Parental home	67 (43%)	44 (28%)
Own or shared tenancy	49 (31%)	72 (46%)
Other relatives	14 (9%)	9 (6%)
Private rented/lodgings	10 (6%)	9 (6%)
Friends	7 (5%)	7 (5%)
No fixed abode	3 (2%)	-
Other	5[27] (3%)	9[28] (6%)
No information	-	5 (3%)
Total	155	155

[27] Hostel (2) caravan (1) owner occupier (1) army barracks (1)
[28] Custody (5) caravan (2) hostel (1) owner occupier (1)

SUMMARY AND CONCLUSIONS

The majority of probation orders had been imposed by the sheriff court under summary proceedings. Just under half contained additional requirements, with the nature of these requirements tending to reflect the availability of services in the study areas. Eighty-two per cent of probationers were male and just under half were between 16 and 20 years of age. Around half the sample had six or more previous convictions when made subject to probation and just under three-fifths had received their orders for offences involving dishonesty. Thirty-eight per cent of probationers were believed by SER authors to have been at risk of a custodial sentence. Family problems, drug and alcohol abuse and mental health problems featured prominently in SERs. Offending was most often attributed to alcohol or drug abuse though in a fifth of cases offenders were said to have been motivated by financial gain and in a similar proportion of cases offending was described as opportunistic or impulsive. In recommending probation to the courts, social workers generally referred to the potential offered by probation to address offending behaviour or behaviour associated with offending; to provide help with practical problems or support of a more general kind; or to capitalise upon the offender's motivation to change. Fifty-nine per cent of orders were completed in full, 14 per cent were discharged early and 25 per cent were breached. There was some evidence that the social circumstances of probationers - in respect of employment and accommodation - had improved over the course of supervision.

The characteristics of probationers varied considerably across the research sites. Probationers in Bruce were more likely to have been ordained to appear for sentence and were less likely to have received probation for offences involving dishonesty. Bruce contained a higher proportion of female offenders and a slightly lower proportion of young offenders than the other two areas. Probationers in Bruce had fewest previous convictions and custodial sentences, were more likely to be first offenders and were less likely to have previous experience of community based social work disposals. They were less likely to have been considered by the SER author as being at risk of custody but were more likely to have additional requirements recommended to the court. Probationers in Bruce were least likely to be breached and most likely to have their orders discharged early. Mental health problems were more often identified among Bruce probationers but alcohol related problems were less evident than in Wallace or Scott. Drug abuse was less likely to be invoked to explain offending while emotional pressure was more often advanced in explanation of offending in this area. Probation was less likely in Bruce to be recommended as a means of addressing offending behaviour and was more likely to be recommended to provide help in relation to employment, education, housing and family relationships and to address violence or aggression.

By contrast, probationers in Wallace had been sentenced for a higher number of offences, had most previous convictions and had served a higher average number of previous custodial sentences. Wallace contained the lowest proportion of first offenders and the highest proportion of persistent offenders. Probationers in Wallace were most likely to be considered at risk of custody and were most likely to be breached. Offending was more likely in Wallace to be explained in terms of financial gain and the provision of help in relation to financial problems was more often advanced than in the other two areas as a reason for recommending probation.

In terms of persistence, probationers in Scott fell somewhere between those in Burns and Wallace, though they in other respects shared more similarities with the latter than with the former. Scott probationers were most likely to have served at least one previous custodial sentence and were most often remanded in custody prior to sentence, while social workers in Scott least often recommended the imposition of additional requirements to probation orders. Alcohol abuse was most often advanced as an explanation for offending in Scott and probation was more often recommended as a means of addressing drug abuse or monitoring the probationer's behaviour.

Whilst conclusions in respect of area differences in practice must remain speculative at this stage, the findings presented in this chapter tend to point to differences in the approaches adopted by social workers across the research sites. More specifically, targeting of probation upon offenders at risk of attracting a custodial sentence and effective gate-keeping as a means of avoiding net-widening (through, for instance, avoiding recommending additional requirements unless these are considered necessary) was less evident in Bruce. Social workers in that area appeared less often to view probation supervision as a vehicle for addressing offending behaviour and more often as a mechanism for accessing practical and personal support for the probationer. As such, it would appear that social workers in Bruce were more often adopting a welfare approach to probation in contrast to those in Scott and Wallace who appeared more often to be operating within a justice model of probation supervision.

In addition to varying across areas, the profiles of probationers differed according to the characteristics of individual offenders. Young offenders were more likely than adults to have been recommended for and to receive a probation order with additional requirements, to have been given probation for an offence involving dishonesty, to have been considered at risk of custody and to have been breached. They were more often than adults described in SERs as having family problems and problems related to low educational achievement. Offending by young probationers was more often described as impulsive or opportunistic, as a response to boredom or as having occurred under the influence of offending peers and they were more likely than adults to be recommended for probation as a means of obtaining help with employment. By contrast, alcohol abuse and medical or mental health problems were more likely to feature among adult offenders and their offending was more likely to be linked to alcohol abuse or emotional pressure. Probation was more likely to be recommended for adults as a means of addressing the abuse of alcohol or drugs.

In comparison with first or early offenders, persistent offenders were more likely to have additional requirements recommended and attached to their probation orders. They were more likely to have been sentenced for a main offence involving dishonesty, were more often considered at risk of custody and were more likely to be breached. Peer group pressure was more often invoked in explanations of offending by first or early offenders and probation was more likely to be recommended for this category of offender as a means of addressing relationship and financial problems. Alcohol and drug abuse more often featured in explanations of offending by persistent offenders and they were more likely than first or early offenders to be recommended for probation to address offending behaviour and drug abuse and to access help in relation to housing and general support.

Probationers who received their orders for main offences involving dishonesty were more likely than those who were sentenced for other types of offences to be recommended for and to receive orders with additional requirements, were more likely to be considered at risk of custody and were more likely to be breached. Financial gain and drug abuse were more often advanced as explanations for offending and probation was more likely to be recommended for this category of offender to address offending behaviour and drug abuse. Offences involving violence or breaches of public order, on the other hand, were more often linked to alcohol abuse, emotional pressures, provocation or self defence. Probation was more likely to be recommended for this category of offender to address alcohol abuse and aggression or violence.

Female probationers were less likely than males to have additional requirements recommended and attached to their probation orders. They were slightly older than men, less likely to be single and more likely to have dependent children living in the same household. Women had fewer previous convictions than men, were more often first offenders and were less likely to have previously served a custodial sentence. Whilst men and women were equally likely to have received probation for offences involving dishonesty, women's offences typically involved theft and fraud while men's offences involved housebreaking and car theft. Women were less likely to be breached than men and were more likely to have their probation orders discharged early on the grounds of satisfactory progress having been made.

Women were more often than men identified as having mental health or emotional problems. Their offending was more likely to be explained in terms of financial gain or as a response to emotional stress and they were more likely than men to be recommended for probation as a means of accessing support of a general kind. In this respect the present findings are similar to those reported by Stewart et al. (1994)[29] in their study of younger offenders under supervision in England and Wales. Male probationers were more often described as having problems relating to alcohol abuse. Their offending was more likely than women's to be linked to alcohol, to be described as opportunistic or impulsive or to have been in response to boredom. Probation was more likely to be recommended for male probationers to address offending behaviour and alcohol abuse.

Clearly, then, the types of probation orders imposed, the nature of offending, the perceived risk of custody and the outcomes of orders varied according to the characteristics of individual probationers. So too did the social and personal problems experienced by probationers, the explanations of their offending advanced by social workers in SERs and the reasons offered in support of probation recommendations. In the following chapter we will examine the process of probation and consider how the packages of services offered differed according to the characteristics of probationers under supervision.

---

[29] Stewart, J., Smith, D. and Stewart, G. (1994) *Understanding Offending Behaviour*, Harlow: Longman.

20

CHAPTER THREE

THE PROCESS AND OUTCOMES OF SUPERVISION

INTRODUCTION

The previous chapter described the characteristics of probationers and the outcomes of their orders. The present chapter examines aspects of the probation process drawing upon information gathered from the case files of 112 probationers: 50 in Wallace, 37 in Scott, 20 in Bruce and five in Burns. This sub-sample of probationers forms the basis of the findings presented in the remainder of the report. As in the previous chapter the cases from Burns are included in discussion of the sample as a whole but, as a consequence of the small numbers involved, are excluded from cross area comparisons which focus instead upon the other three research sites.

The criteria adopted to select probation cases for more in-depth analysis have been described in Chapter One. Cases were excluded if the order was imposed by a court other than the sheriff court in the study area. In Scott and Wallace cases were, additionally, excluded if they were imposed upon first offenders in respect of an offence carrying a gravity rating of less than three. As such, in those areas with a higher throughput of probation orders the research focused upon probation cases prioritised by the National Standards - offenders who might otherwise have been at risk of attracting a custodial sentence.

Most cases were excluded from the more detailed analysis of the probation process not because they were lower tariff but because the probation orders had been imposed by courts other than the sheriff courts in the study areas. Nineteen cases were excluded because the probation orders were imposed by sheriff courts outwith the study areas; 14 because they were imposed by courts other than sheriff courts; and ten because they were made in respect of first offenders who were being sentenced for an offence carrying a gravity rating of less than three. Therefore, despite the fact that some lower tariff cases were excluded in two of the study areas, this group of probationers was virtually indistinguishable from the larger sample from which it was drawn. As such the findings presented in this and in subsequent chapters can be considered reasonably representative of probation practice in the study areas.

Between-area differences which were highlighted in Chapter Two were also evident in the smaller sample and need only be summarised here. There was no significant difference in the average age of probationers across the different areas, though there were slightly fewer young offenders in Bruce than in Scott and Wallace (45 per cent compared with 59 and 54 per cent respectively) and there was a higher proportion of female probationers in Bruce (30 per cent compared with 14 per cent in Scott and 12 per cent in Wallace).

The majority of probationers in Bruce (80 per cent) had been ordained to appear for sentence while this was true of just 32 per cent in Scott and Wallace. There was no difference in the average gravity rating of the main offences for which probationers received their orders, though offenders in Bruce were less likely than those in Scott or Wallace to have received orders in excess of 12 months (15 per cent compared with 32 per cent and 28 per cent). The average length of probation order did not, however, differ significantly across the research sites, being 14.4 months in Bruce, 14.0 months in Scott and 15.4 months in Wallace. Probationers in Bruce were slightly less likely to have been subject to supervision through the children's hearing system (40 per cent compared with 49 per cent in Scott and 52 per cent in Wallace) and were less likely to have previous experience of community based social work disposals (35 per cent compared with 57 and 56 per cent).

Probationers in Wallace had the highest average number of previous convictions (10.7) and those in Bruce the lowest (3.5). Probationers in Scott had, on average, 7.5 convictions prior to receiving their probation orders. Probationers in Wallace were most likely to have ten or more previous convictions (58 per cent compared with 49 per cent in Scott and 30 per cent in Bruce). Probationers in Scott were most likely to have served at least one custodial sentence (43 per cent compared with 32 per cent in Wallace and 10 per cent in Bruce) but probationers in Wallace had served, on average, more previous custodial sentences than probationers in Bruce or Scott (2.6 compared with 0.1 and 1.6). Finally probationers in Wallace were most likely to have been considered by the SER author as being at risk of attracting a custodial sentence (51 per cent compared with 23 per cent in Scott and 11 per cent in Bruce). Probationers in Bruce were more likely than those in Scott or Wallace not to be thought at risk of custody (67 per cent compared with 30 per cent and 37 per cent). Taken together, then, these findings suggest that Bruce was dealing, on average, with lower tariff probationers while social workers in Wallace were working with offenders who were slightly higher tariff, on average, than those in Scott.

CONTACT WITH PROBATIONERS DURING THEIR ORDERS

The frequency and location of interviews

The National Standards require that "offenders sentenced to probation must be seen by their designated supervisor as soon as possible and not later than one week after the order is made" (SWSG, 1991, para. 62.1). An average of 8.2 days elapsed between the order being imposed and the first interview with the probationer. Sixty-seven per cent of probationers were first seen within one week of sentencing, with 21 per cent being seen on the same day that the order was imposed. A further 20 per cent of cases were seen within 14 days, while more than two weeks elapsed prior to the initial contact in 13 per cent of cases.

There was, as Table 3.1 illustrates, some difference across the three research sites in the average time which elapsed prior to the first appointment with the probationer and in the proportions of probationers seen within one week of the order being made, though these differences were not statistically reliable. It is clear from Table 3.1, however, that the National Standards were not being met in respect of the timing of initial interviews in a substantial proportion of cases in each area and, indeed, in as many as half the cases in Bruce. Case notes in files suggested that, where National Standards were not being met, this was usually because the offender failed to keep the initial appointment or, in a smaller proportion of cases, because the probationer was remanded in custody for other offences. It is also possible that in Bruce initial appointments were sometimes more difficult to arrange within the specified time-scale because of the rural nature of the area.

Table 3.1: Time to first appointment by area

	Bruce (n=20)	Scott[30] (n=35)	Wallace[31] (n=48)
Average no. of days to first appointment	9.7	6.7	8.8
Percentage of probationers seen within one week	50	69	73

The National Standards also specify the frequency of appointments at different stages of the probation process. More specifically, there is an expectation that probationers will be seen on eight occasions in the first three months (weekly in the first month and fortnightly thereafter) with two of these appointments taking place in the offender's home. After this initial phase of supervision appointments should take place on at least a monthly basis.

Taking into account only those cases (71 in total) which resulted in successful completion or early discharge in Bruce, Scott and Wallace, across the sample as a whole there were an average of 7.5 contacts with the offender during the first three months of the probation order. As Table 3.2 indicates, the average number of contacts was lower overall in Bruce than in the other two areas and in Bruce there were significantly fewer office based appointments with the probationer. Social workers in Bruce, however, made more home visits to probationers. Indeed, probationers in Bruce were, on average, more likely to be seen by their social worker at home as opposed to the social work office. Home visits may offer advantages over office contacts in two main respects: first, they may provide an opportunity for insight into the probationer's home circumstances and their manner of responding outwith the unnatural environment of a social work office; second, they may offer more opportunity for informal contact with other family members which may further help to contextualise the probationer's offending and serve to engage other significant individuals in the probation process.

Table 3.2: Average number and location of visits in the first 3 months

	Office contacts	Home visits	Total
Bruce	2.1	3.5	5.6
Scott	6.2	2.0	8.2
Wallace	6.5	1.8	8.3

The average number of appointments at which other family members were also present and the number involving the offender alone are summarised in Table 3.3. It is clear that although social workers in Bruce made more home visits, these were, in the main, conducted with the offender alone. The highest average number of contacts with other family members present was recorded in Wallace.

---

[30] Data unavailable in two cases.
[31] Data unavailable in two cases.

Table 3.3: Average number of visits in first three months with offenders and other family members

	Offender only	Offender and family	Total
Bruce	5.1	0.5	5.6
Scott	7.7	0.5	8.2
Wallace	7.2	1.1	8.3

The actual number of contacts with probationers during the first three months of the order is summarised by area in Table 3.4. In Burns, three probationers were seen on seven occasions and two were seen eight or more times. Overall, the number of contacts with probationers met the National Standard in fewer than half the cases (44 per cent). The Standard was met most often in Scott and least often in Bruce where only one of the 20 probationers was seen on the specified number of occasions.

Table 3.4: Number of contacts in the first three months by area

	Bruce	Scott	Wallace	Total
Four to five	10 (53%)	3 (11%)	2 (8%)	15 (21%)
Six to seven	8 (42%)	7 (26%	10 (40%)	25 (35%)
Eight or more	1 (5%)	17 (63%)	13 (52%)	31 (44%)
Total	19	27	25	71

Probation orders in Bruce were, however, most likely to meet the Standard in respect of having two home visits within the initial three month period. Seventy-nine percent of probationers in Bruce had two or more home visits compared with 48 per cent in Scott and 28 per cent in Wallace. Only one of the five probationers in Burns had two or more home visits in the first three months. Overall, 47 per cent of probation orders met the Standard in this respect. Twenty-four per cent of probationers, however, had no home visits during the first three months of their order.

Although Bruce had the lowest average number of contacts in the first three months, it had slightly more contacts in the remainder of the first year of supervision than did Scott and Wallace. As in the first three months, a significant proportion of these contacts took place in the offender's home (Table 3.5).

Table 3.5: Average number and location of visits in the rest of the first year

	Office contacts	Home visits	Total
Bruce	5.6	5.1	10.6
Scott	6.7	2.4	9.1
Wallace	7.7	1.8	9.5

The average number of home and office contacts per probation order are summarised by area in Table 3.6. There was no significant difference in the total number of contacts across study areas though probationers in Scott and Wallace were most often seen in the social work office while those in Bruce were, on average, seen as often at home as in the office.

Table 3.6: Average number of home and office contacts per probation order

	Office contacts	Home visits	Total
Bruce	9.3	9.4	18.7
Scott	13.7	4.8	18.5
Wallace	16.5	3.9	20.4

As would be expected, the number of contacts with the probationer varied according to the length of the order. Taking into account only those orders that were completed successfully and which were not discharged early, there was a clear association between length of order and the total number of contacts with the probationer. Orders of six to nine months had an average of 9.3 contacts with the probationer; those of 12

months had an average of 12.6; 18 month orders had, on average, 20.4 contacts; and orders of more than 18 months had an average of 23.4. The number of contacts by length of probation order are summarised in Table 3.7.

Table 3.7: Number of contacts by length of order

Number of contacts	6-9 months	12 months	18 months	>18 months	Total
0-10	3	1	-	-	4
11-20	8	24	1	1	34
21-30	-	10	4	2	16
31-40	-	-	-	5	5
Total	11	35	5	8	59

Reviews

The National Standards specify that formal reviews of progress, involving the participation of the offender, should be carried out at three and six months and, where the length of the order permits, six monthly thereafter. The purpose of the review is to establish what progress has been made towards meeting the targets identified in the action plan and identify tasks and goals for the next period of supervision. It should also set out both the required frequency of contact and the venue at which contact will take place.

First reviews were conducted, on average, within 15.5 weeks of the probation order being made. The average number of weeks which had elapsed prior to the initial review was 18.5 in Bruce, 15.8 in Scott and 13.7 in Wallace.

As Table 3.8 shows, initial reviews were conducted within the first 14 weeks of the order in 51 per cent of cases, though there were variations across the study areas in the proportion of initial reviews which met the National Standard in this respect. Wallace had the highest proportion of reviews conducted within 14 weeks, with two-thirds of the initial reviews being conducted within that period of time. Bruce, on the other hand, had the highest proportion of reviews conducted 14 weeks or more after the probation order was initially imposed.

It is possible that reviews are more difficult to arrange in rural areas which might involve the offender travelling some distance to the local social work office. Alternatively, it was suggested by a manager that social workers in Bruce were somewhat resistant to the concept of National Standards in general and reviews in particular. Reluctance on the part of social workers to convene formal reviews may be reflected in the present finding.

Table 3.8: Time until first review by area[32]

	Bruce	Scott	Wallace	Total
Less than 14 weeks	7 (37%)	15 (44%)	20 (67%)	42 (51%)
14 or more weeks	12 (63%)	19 (56%)	10 (33%)	41 (49%)

The number of reviews conducted in three of the study areas are summarised in Table 3.9. In Burns, four cases were reviewed on two occasions and one was subject to a third review. The most striking difference between the study areas relates to the relatively high proportion of cases in Wallace in which no reviews were recorded and, conversely, the relatively low proportion of cases which were subject to formal review on three or more occasions. The latter cannot be accounted for by the differing lengths of orders across areas for, as we have already seen, the length of order did not vary markedly in the three research sites. It is possible that reviews did take place at a similar frequency as in the other areas but that these were often not recorded in case files. A more likely explanation, however, is that reviews did not occur or occurred relatively infrequently as a consequence of higher levels of non-compliance and breach in Wallace. As we shall see later in this chapter, Wallace, with its higher proportion of more persistent offenders, issued formal warnings in a higher proportion of cases and returned more offenders to court for further offending or failure to comply.

---

[32] Excludes 24 cases in which no reviews were recorded in the file

Table 3.9: Number of probation reviews by area

	Bruce	Scott	Wallace	Total
None recorded	1	3	20	24
1	1	4	10	15
2	8	11	13	32
3	5	15	3	23
4 or more	5	4	4	13
Total	20	37	50	107

Some support for this explanation is provided by the finding that 59 per cent of probation orders that were breached had no reviews conducted: this compares with only five per cent of orders that were completed successfully and six per cent that were subject to early discharge. Orders that were discharged early were most likely to have been reviewed on four or more occasions (24 per cent compared with 13 per cent of completed orders and 3 per cent of breaches) reflecting, no doubt, the fact early discharge was more likely to be sought in respect of longer probation orders. There was, however, no clear association between the number of reviews held and the number of formal warnings issued to probationers.

A total of 210 reviews were identified in case files. The majority were attended by the social worker alone (95) or by the social worker and senior social worker (91)[33]. Student social workers were present in addition to the social worker and senior in two cases. Twenty-two reviews involved the participation of other individuals who had an interest in the case. Intensive probation project staff were known to have been involved in 12 reviews and key-workers from supported accommodation projects were involved in four others. Community service staff attended three reviews, community psychiatric nurses attended two and drug and alcohol counsellors each attended one review. None of the nine reviews in Burns was attended by staff from other agencies. There were only minor variations in the representation of other individuals at reviews in the other three areas: 7 per cent of reviews in Bruce, 10 per cent in Scott and 15 per cent in Wallace were attended by other individuals with an interest in the case.

There were, however, striking differences between the areas in terms of the proportion of reviews which were attended by senior social workers. Senior social workers are required to attend reviews if it is in the interests of good case management or if requested to do so by the probationer. Senior social workers attended the majority of reviews in Scott (92 per cent) but only a minority of reviews in Bruce (13 per cent) and Wallace (14 per cent) were conducted with the senior social worker present. Six of the nine reviews recorded in Burns were attended by the senior social worker.

It is impossible to know what significance to attach to the senior social worker's absence from reviews. The policy adopted in Scott was that first line managers should normally attend reviews in the interests of good case management, but the impact that this had upon the effectiveness of probation supervision, and therefore, the necessity of their presence at all reviews - particularly if the social worker is experienced - is difficult to discern. The impression gained by the researchers was that case files in Scott were more systematic and better organised than those in the other study areas, a practice which might have been prompted by the line manager's regular involvement in reviews and by the regular sampling of probation files by managers to monitor the quality of practice and adherence to National Standards.

The outcome of the majority of reviews (179 or 89 per cent) was that there be no change to the action plan. The action plan was changed in ten reviews while the decision in four reviews was to apply for a variation of the order (the attachment or removal of additional requirements). In 17 reviews a decision was taken to apply for early discharge of the probation order.

There was a relationship between the outcome of reviews and the level of compliance by the probationer (as evidenced by the number of formal warnings issued during the order). In 12 of the 17 cases in which an application for early discharge was recommended the probationer had received no formal warnings (one indicator of progress having been made during the period of supervision). In three of the four cases in which a decision was made to apply for a variation of the order, by contrast, the probationer had received two or more formal warnings from the supervising social worker.

In total five applications were made to amend the original probation order, all of which were successful. Early discharge of the probation order was sought in 18 cases and granted in all but one.

---

[33] In some cases it was not possible to tell from case files whether the first line manager was actually present at the review or simply signed the review form.

THE PROCESS OF SUPERVISION

It was possible from case files to identify the areas of work specified by social workers in action plans, other issues which emerged during the process of supervision, and the nature of services provided. It is possible, of course, that other work was undertaken with probationers which was not recorded in files. The findings reported in this section are, therefore, dependent upon the accuracy with which the supervision process was recorded in files and the extent to which detailed information about the nature of intervention was provided.

Issues identified in action plans and during supervision

Table 3.10 summarises the issues identified by social workers in action plans and the frequency with which different issues emerged additionally during the process of supervising the probationer.

Action plans (whether developed at the SER stage or following the imposition of the probation order) were evident in all but three cases in Wallace and one in Burns, though they were rarely produced as a document in their own right with the consequence that there was, in effect, no clear contractual arrangement between the social worker and probationer.

The offending behaviour itself featured most commonly in action plans. Personal relationships and employment also featured in more than half the cases in the sample while financial problems, accommodation, alcohol and drugs were identified as issues in between a third and a half of all probation orders. Employment, accommodation and financial problems were most likely to emerge as additional areas for attention which had not previously been identified for inclusion in the probation action plan.

Table 3.10: Issues identified in action plans and during the course of supervision

Issue	In action plan		Identified during supervision		Total (n=112)	
Offending	82	(73%)	4	(4%)	86	(77%)
Relationships	56	(50%)	10	(9%)	66	(59%)
Employment	40	(36%)	20	(18%)	60	(54%)
Accommodation	26	(23%)	22	(20%)	48	(43%)
Financial	29	(26%)	18	(18%)	47	(42%)
Alcohol	32	(29%)	8	(7%)	40	(36%)
Drugs	29	(26%)	8	(7%)	37	(33%)
Leisure time	17	(15%)	9	(8%)	26	(23%)
Social skills	14	(12%)	8	(7%)	22	(20%)
Physical/mental health	12	(11%)	9	(8%)	21	(19%)
Violence	11	(10%)	4	(4%)	15	(13%)
Education	11	(10%)	2	(2%)	13	(12%)
Other[34]	10	(9%)	8	(7%)	18	(16%)

The content of action plans differed across the research sites. Plans in Bruce were less likely than those in Scott or Wallace to contain explicit reference to addressing offending behaviour (35 per cent compared with 78 per cent and 82 per cent), addressing alcohol use (15 per cent compared with 32 per cent and 26 per cent) and providing help with financial problems (15 per cent compared with 30 per cent and 28 per cent). They were more likely, on the other hand, to include relationship issues (70 per cent compared with 38 per cent in Scott and 48 per cent in Wallace) and medical or mental health issues (30 per cent compared with 5 per cent and 6 per cent). Action plans in Scott were less likely than those in Bruce or Wallace to contain reference to employment (27 per cent compared with 40 per cent in each of the other 2 areas). Finally, less emphasis was placed in Wallace upon addressing the probationer's use of leisure time (6 per cent of cases compared with 30 per cent in Bruce and 19 per cent in Scott).

The areas most commonly identified in action plans in Bruce were relationships (70 per cent), employment (40 per cent), offending behaviour (35 per cent), use of leisure time, medical or mental health problems and

---

34 Includes child care, bereavement and racism

drugs (30 per cent each). Offending featured most often in Scott (78 per cent of plans) followed by relationships (38 per cent), alcohol use (32 per cent) and financial problems and drug use (30 per cent each). Offending (82 per cent), relationships (48 per cent), employment (40 per cent) and financial problems (28 per cent) predominated in Wallace.

The content of action plans was found to differ according to the characteristics of individual offenders. Turning first to age differences, action plans made in respect of young offenders (that is, those under 21 years of age) were more likely than those made in respect of older offenders to include offending behaviour (85 per cent compared with 60 per cent), employment (47 per cent compared with 23 per cent) and accommodation (29 per cent compared with 17 per cent). This suggests that social workers generally recognised the importance of tackling offending behaviour among the younger age group who are identified as a priority category in the National Objectives and Standards. It also points to the greater tendency for younger offenders to have significant practical problems (Stewart et al., 1994). Action plans developed in respect of older offenders were more likely to focus upon alcohol abuse (41 per cent compared with 17 per cent), medical or mental health problems (17 per cent compared with 5 per cent) and violence (17 per cent compared with 3 per cent). The most common issues contained in the action plans for young offenders were offending behaviour (85 per cent), relationships (49 per cent), employment (47 per cent), accommodation and financial problems (29 per cent each). Offending behaviour (60 per cent), relationships (51 per cent), alcohol abuse (41 per cent) and drug abuse (28 per cent) were the issues most often included in the action plans of older offenders.

Some differences were also observed between the action plans of first or early offenders (those with up to two previous convictions) and those of persistent offenders (those with six or more previous convictions when made subject to probation). The latter were more likely to contain reference to alcohol related problems (35 per cent compared with 16 per cent), drug related problems (32 per cent compared with 19 per cent), social skills (14 per cent compared with 6 per cent) and violence (14 per cent compared with 3 per cent). The former were more likely to include relationship difficulties (59 per cent compared with 47 per cent) and accommodation (28 per cent compared with 19 per cent). Offending behaviour figured equally prominently in the action plans of early and persistent offenders, being included in 75 per cent of plans. The issues most commonly contained in the action plans of first or early offenders were offending behaviour (75 per cent), relationships (59 per cent), employment (31 per cent), accommodation and financial problems (28 per cent each). Offending behaviour (75 per cent), relationships (47 per cent), alcohol (35 per cent), employment (33 per cent) and drugs (32 per cent) were the issues most frequently included in the action plans of persistent offenders.

Gender differences were also evident in action plans. Plans pertaining to male offenders were more likely to include reference to alcohol abuse (30 per cent of male compared with 22 per cent of females), drug abuse (28 per cent compared with 17 per cent), employment (37 per cent compared with 28 per cent), use of leisure time[35] (17 per cent compared with 6 per cent) and, most markedly, offending behaviour (77 per cent compared with 50 per cent). Women's action plans, on the other hand, more often identified accommodation (33 per cent compared with 21 per cent), education (17 per cent compared with 8 per cent) and financial problems (39 per cent compared with 23 per cent). The issues which featured most often in the action plans of male probationers were offending (77 per cent), relationships (51 per cent), employment (37 per cent), alcohol (30 per cent) and drugs (28 per cent). Those identified most frequently in female probationers' action plans were offending (50 per cent), relationships (44 per cent) financial problems (39 per cent), accommodation (33 per cent) and employment (28 per cent).

There were, finally, clear differences in the content of action plans according to the type of offence in respect of which the probation order was imposed. In analysing action plans by the nature of the main offence, the following three groupings were employed: offences involving dishonesty; offences involving violence or breaches of public order; and all other offences (which included small numbers of probationers who had been convicted of a variety of offences including road traffic offences, drug offences, criminal damage and, in one case, a sexual offence). For the sake of brevity, the three groups will be referred to as "dishonesty", "conduct" and "other".

Action plans in respect of "dishonesty" offenders were most likely to include offending behaviour (83 per cent compared with 67 per cent and 50 per cent of "conduct" and "other" offenders respectively) and employment (42 per cent compared with 26 and 30 per cent). Action plans relating to "conduct" offenders were most likely to contain reference to alcohol (52 per cent compared with 18 per cent of "dishonesty" offenders and 30 per cent of "other" offenders), to medical or mental health problems (22 per cent compared with 6 per cent and 10 per cent) and violence (30 per cent compared with 3 per cent and 5 per cent). Action plans in

---

[35] This may reflect a greater influence of peer group on the offending of (in particular young) males.

respect of the mixed category of "other" offenders were most likely to identify accommodation (35 per cent compared with 25 per cent of "dishonesty" offenders and 11 per cent of "conduct" offenders), education (30 per cent compared with 5 per cent and 7 per cent) and other miscellaneous issues (25 per cent compared with 3 per cent and 11 per cent). The issues most often contained in the action plans of "dishonesty" offenders were offending behaviour (83 per cent), relationships (43 per cent), employment (42 per cent) and financial problems (28 per cent). Those most commonly found in the action plans of "conduct" offenders were offending (67 per cent), alcohol (52 per cent), relationships (52 per cent) and violence (30 per cent). Finally, the action plans of "other" offenders were most likely to focus upon relationships (55 per cent), offending behaviour (50 per cent) and accommodation (35 per cent). It would appear, therefore, that action plans were, particularly in the case of offenders convicted of offences involving dishonesty, violence or breaches of public order, tailored to a significant extent to the issues which might be assumed to underlie the offending behaviour.

Services provided to probationers

As Table 3.11 indicates, intervention aimed at directly addressing offending behaviour featured in 70 per cent of cases and was more likely than other areas of intervention to involve groupwork or a combination of group and individual work. The most striking feature of Table 3.11, however, is the finding that the majority of work with probationers was undertaken by social workers or by other agencies on a one-to one-basis. It should be noted that Tables 3.11 and 3.12 do not include services provided by intensive probation projects. These are discussed later in this section.

Table 3.11: Services provided and nature of intervention

Type of service	Individual	Group	Both	Total (n=112)
Offending	70	4	5	79 (70%)
Relationships	54	-	-	54 (48%)
Employment	47	2	1	50 (45%)
Financial	42	-	-	42 (38%)
Accommodation	41	-	-	41 (37%)
Alcohol	35	2	1	38 (34%)
Drugs	33	2	1	36 (32%)
Leisure	20	2	1	23 (20%)
Physical/mental health	20	1	-	21 (19%)
Social skills	18	-	-	18 (16%)
Violence	15	-	-	15 (13%)
Other	9	1	-	10 (9%)

Table 3.12 summarises services provided by social workers and by other statutory or voluntary agencies. Clearly the majority of work undertaken with offenders on probation was undertaken by the supervising social workers themselves. It also appeared from files that if other agencies became involved in a case, they usually assumed sole responsibility for providing the particular service concerned. Use was most often made of other agencies in the provision of services related to employment, alcohol or drugs and health issues. Intervention which focused upon relationships, financial problems, the acquisition of social skills and violence was, without exception, undertaken exclusively by the supervising social worker. Social workers also, with few exceptions, were solely responsible for dealing with offenders' accommodation problems and for helping offenders to make more constructive use of their leisure time.

Independent sector service providers in the four study areas who were interviewed in the context of the present research programme were unanimously agreed that in general their relationships with the local authority social work department were good and had, indeed, improved since the introduction of 100 per cent funding and the creation of specialist arrangements for service delivery. A complaint voiced by some, however, was that a considerable amount of effort was required on the part of the independent sector to ensure that social work practitioners were aware of and, more importantly, made use of the services they provided.

Table 3.12: Services provided and service providers

Type of service	Social worker	Other agency	Social worker and other agency	Total (n=112)	
Offending	76	1	2	79	(70%)
Relationships	54	-	-	54	(48%)
Employment	32	18	-	50	(45%)
Financial	42	-	-	42	(38%)
Accommodation	40	1	-	41	(37%)
Alcohol	29	8	1	38	(34%)
Drugs	26	9	1	36	(32%)
Leisure	21	2	-	23	(20%)
Physical/mental health	13	8	-	21	(19%)
Social skills	18	-	-	18	(16%)
Violence	15	-	-	15	(13%)
Other	8	2	-	10	(9%)

Seventeen offenders were made subject to probation orders with the additional requirement that they attend an intensive probation project. Work undertaken by intensive projects was generally not recorded in any detail in probation case files. From what information was available it appeared that, other than addressing offending behaviour itself - which is the primary focus of programmes of this kind - intensive projects were most likely to focus additionally upon the use of drugs or alcohol (7 and 5 cases respectively), the offender's use of leisure time (8 cases) and personal relationships (7 cases). The scope of the present study precluded the examination of intensive probation project records, thereby preventing a fuller discussion of their contribution to the probation process[36]. One interviewee from an intensive probation project commented that supervising social workers were reluctant to engage in joint work when probationers were attending intensive projects and expressed a hope that more participative arrangements could be developed. In another area, however, supervising social workers participated actively in intensive probation reviews and appeared to have established good working relationships with project staff. This project, interestingly, was provided by the local authority rather than by the independent sector. Whilst it is impossible to draw any conclusions on the basis of the experience of two projects, it is possible to speculate that mistrust or resentment of independent sector provision (especially where independent sector providers are seen as undertaking the more "interesting" areas of probation work) might, in some instances, militate against the development of more collaborative working methods.

Before concluding our discussion of the services provided to probationers in the sample, it is worth noting that the types of services provided differed by area and according to the characteristics of individual offenders. Addressing offending behaviour was more often identified in Scott (84 per cent of cases) than in Bruce (65 per cent) or Wallace (62 per cent). Social workers in Scott were also more likely to focus upon alcohol use (38 per cent compared with 32 per cent in Wallace and 25 per cent in Bruce), financial problems (49 per cent compared with 38 per cent and 25 per cent) and social skills (24 per cent compared with 12 per cent and 10 per cent). Social workers in Bruce were more likely than those in Scott or Wallace to focus upon relationship issues (65 per cent compared with 43 per cent and 44 per cent respectively), the probationer's use of leisure time (50 per cent compared with 22 per cent and 6 per cent) and medical or mental health issues (40 per cent compared with 11 per cent and 14 per cent). Finally, supervising social workers in Wallace were less likely than those in Bruce or Scott to address accommodation problems (30 per cent compared with 45 per cent and 46 per cent), drugs (24 per cent compared with 35 per cent and 45 per cent) and employment (34 per cent compared with 55 per cent and 57 per cent).

The issues most often focused upon in Bruce were relationships (65 per cent), offending (65 per cent), employment (55 per cent) and use of leisure time (50 per cent). The focus of intervention in Scott was most commonly offending (84 per cent), employment (57 per cent), financial problems (49 per cent) and accommodation (46 per cent). In Wallace, offending behaviour (62 per cent), relationships (44 per cent),

---

[36] The Social Work Research Centre at the University of Stirling is currently completing an evaluation of intensive probation projects, two of which are located in the study areas included in the present research. This will complement the present study by providing a detailed account of the operation and impact of intensive probation provision.

financial problems (38 per cent) and employment (34 per cent) were most likely to feature as the focus for service provision by social workers or other agencies. The relative emphasis upon offending behaviour in the different study areas warrants some additional comment. In particular, offending featured in 82 per cent of action plans in Wallace, but was focused upon directly in only 62 per cent of cases. The high breach rate in Wallace offers a likely explanation: often orders were returned to court for non-compliance or as a result of further offending before any work could effectively be undertaken.

Social workers were more likely when supervising young offenders (as opposed to those aged 21 years or older) to focus upon offending (79 per cent compared with 62 per cent) and employment (60 per cent compared with 28 per cent). Intervention with older offenders was more likely to address alcohol abuse (45 per cent compared with 24 per cent), medical or mental health problems (32 per cent compared with 7 per cent), relationships (55 per cent compared with 43 per cent) and violence (21 per cent compared with 7 per cent). The services most often provided to young offenders related to offending behaviour (79 per cent), employment (60 per cent), relationships (43 per cent) and financial problems (40 per cent). Those most often provided to older offenders focused upon offending behaviour (62 per cent), relationships (55 per cent), alcohol (45 per cent) and accommodation (40 per cent).

Work with first or early offenders was more likely than that undertaken with persistent offenders to address offending behaviour (81 per cent compared with 68 per cent), relationships (60 per cent compared with 45 per cent), financial problems (47 per cent compared with 38 per cent) and use of leisure time (31 per cent compared with 23 per cent). Intervention with persistent offenders was more likely to focus upon alcohol abuse (43 per cent compared with 25 per cent), drug abuse (34 per cent compared with 22 per cent) and violence (16 per cent compared with 9 per cent). The issues most often addressed with first or early offenders were offending behaviour (81 per cent), relationships (60 per cent), employment (56 per cent) and financial problems (47 per cent). In the case of persistent offenders, offending behaviour (68 per cent), employment (58 per cent), relationships (45 per cent) and alcohol abuse (43 per cent) predominated in terms of the social work service offered.

The pattern of service provision to these two different groups of offenders merits further comment. In particular, it may seem surprising that social workers were less likely, in the case of persistent offenders, to focus upon offending behaviour. This group would, however, be more likely to attend intensive probation projects with an explicit focus upon offending behaviour and supervising social workers may, as a consequence, have decided to focus their attention on other areas of work. The services provided to first or early offenders are suggestive of a preventive approach on the part of social workers: addressing directly both the offending behaviour and other circumstances which might make further offending more likely. Work with persistent offenders was apparently more likely to focus on often deeply entrenched personal problems which contributed to continued offending behaviour.

There were also clear gender differences in the pattern of service provision. Intervention with male probationers was more likely to focus upon offending behaviour (73 per cent compared with 61 per cent), employment (49 per cent compared with 22 per cent) and drugs (33 per cent compared with 22 per cent). Work undertaken with female probationers, on the other hand, was more likely to address accommodation (56 per cent compared with 33 per cent), financial problems (56 per cent compared with 36 per cent), medical or mental health problems (39 per cent compared with 15 per cent), social skills (28 per cent compared with 14 per cent), violence (22 per cent compared with 12 per cent) and "other problems" (33 per cent compared with four per cent). The latter category consisted entirely of child care issues.

The main areas of work undertaken with male probationers were offending behaviour (73 per cent), employment (49 per cent), relationships (48 per cent) and financial problems (36 per cent). Social workers were most likely to address offending behaviour (61 per cent), financial problems (56 per cent), accommodation (56 per cent) and relationships (50 per cent) in their work with female probationers.

Turning finally to our three categories of main offence type (as described earlier in this chapter) relatively few differences in the nature of services provided emerged. There was little difference, for example, in the percentage of cases in which offending behaviour was addressed (72 per cent, 67 per cent and 75 per cent in the case of "dishonesty", "conduct" and "other" offenders respectively). "Dishonesty" offenders were, however, more likely to receive services related to financial problems (42 per cent compared with 33 per cent of "conduct" offenders and '35 per cent of "other" offenders). Work with "conduct" offenders was more likely to include intervention focused upon alcohol abuse (59 per cent compared with 23 per cent of "dishonesty" offenders and 35 per cent of "other" offenders), medical or mental health problems (37 per cent compared with 11 per cent and 20 per cent), relationships (63 per cent compared with 44 per cent and 45 per cent) and violence (37 per cent compared with two per cent and 20 per cent). Work with "other" offenders was more likely to focus upon drug abuse[37] (40 per cent compared with 30 per cent of "dishonesty" and "conduct" offenders) and education (20 per cent compared with 2 per cent and 7 per cent).

---

[37] It will be recalled that drug offences were included within this broad category.

There were clear differences in the relative prominence of different services across offence categories. In the case of "dishonesty" offenders, the types of intervention most commonly provided were offending behaviour (72 per cent), employment (47 per cent), relationships (44 per cent), financial problems (42 per cent) and accommodation (41 per cent). Much of the focus, therefore, was on practical problems which might be assumed to have contributed directly or indirectly to the offending behaviour. "Conduct" offenders most often received services focused upon offending behaviour (67 per cent), relationships (63 per cent), alcohol abuse (59 per cent), employment (41 per cent) and violence (37 per cent). Again, therefore, there is some evidence that the nature of service provision was tailored to factors which may be assumed to contribute to that type of offending behaviour. "Other" offenders were most likely to receive services focused on offending behaviour (75 per cent), relationships (45 per cent), employment (45 per cent) and drugs (40 per cent). In view of the disparate nature of offences included in this category it is not possible, however, to comment further on the apparent relevance or otherwise of services provided to this group of probationers.

In 66 per cent of cases (74) the same social worker was responsible for supervision throughout the probation order. Twenty-three per cent of probationers (26) experienced one change of social worker while nine probationers (8 per cent) had three different social workers during their orders and three offenders (3 per cent) had four. The majority of changes (24) occurred because the supervising social worker left the office. On seven occasions a new social worker was allocated to a case which had been supervised by a student whose placement with the agency had ended. In only one instance was a change of social worker instigated as a result of a "clash of personalities" between the probationer and the supervising officer.

There were wide variations in the numbers of supervising social workers across the research sites. In Scott, for example, 59 per cent of probationers experienced at least one change of social worker during their orders: 13 probationers had two supervising social workers, six had three and three had four. This compares with Bruce where 85 per cent of probationers had no change of social worker and Wallace where no change of social worker occurred in 78 per cent of cases. Only one probationer in Wallace and two in Bruce had three different social workers during the currency of their order and no probationers in these areas had their social worker changed three times. During the fieldwork period Scott suffered staff shortages as a consequence of illness and maternity leave: senior social workers often took over the supervision of a probation case in the interim or until it could be re-allocated.

OBJECTIVES AND THEIR ACHIEVEMENT

In each case included in the sample an attempt was made to identify up to four main objectives in the case and to assess the extent to which they had been achieved. Where possible, reference was made both to the case notes and to the probation completion report contained in the case file. The latter were, however, often unavailable, particularly where analysis of files took place shortly after the termination of the order and prior to the completion of final reports. Those which were available did tend to refer back to the issues identified in the original SER and to indicate, from the social worker's perspective, the extent to which objectives had been achieved. The researchers' assessment of objectives and their achievement was therefore based upon a variable quality and amount of relevant material, a caveat which should be borne in mind when considering the following discussion.

In two cases (one in Burns and one in Wallace) no clear objectives could be identified from case files. Twelve per cent of cases appeared to have one objective, 46 per cent had two objectives 25 per cent had three objectives and 15 per cent had at least four. Two of the remaining four files in Burns contained reference to two objectives and four objectives were identifiable in two others. The majority of cases in Bruce and Scott had either two or three objectives (90 per cent and 82 per cent respectively). This was also true in Wallace where 64 per cent of cases had either two or three objectives. In this study area, however, four or more objectives were identified in 25 per cent of cases.

Table 3.13 summarises the objectives identified from files in Bruce, Scott and Wallace. Tackling offending appeared to feature as an explicit objective in 57 per cent of cases, though it may have been an implicit objective in others, with offending being addressed indirectly through the resolution of other issues. Tackling offending behaviour was an explicit objective in only 25 per cent of cases in Bruce compared with 65 and 63 per cent in Scott and Wallace. By comparison, objectives linked to the amelioration of family relationships and the personal development of the offender featured more prominently in Bruce than in the other two areas.

The most commonly identified objectives in Burns were employment, drugs, family relationships, personal development and offending, in that order. In Scott they were offending, alcohol, drugs and financial problems while in Wallace offending, employment, alcohol and drugs were the objectives most commonly identified from social work case files. In other words, it appeared that the primary objectives of work with individual probationers in Scott and Wallace were more likely to be focused upon offending behaviour and other factors directly linked to offending. In Bruce, on the other hand, the pattern of objectives identified is suggestive of social workers adopting more of a welfare approach to probation supervision.

Table 3.13: Objectives identified by area

	Bruce (n=20)	Scott (n=37)	Wallace (n=49)	Total (n=106)
Offending	5 (25%)	24 (65%)	31 (63%)	60 (57%)
Employment/education	9 (45%)	5 (14%)	18 (38%)	32 (30%)
Alcohol	2 (10%)	11 (30%)	14 (29%)	27 (26%)
Drugs	6 (30%)	11 (30%)	10 (20%)	27 (26%)
Family relationships	6 (30%)	5 (14%)	7 (14%)	18 (17%)
Financial	2 (10%)	6 (16%)	8 (16%)	16 (15%)
Accommodation	2 (10%)	4 (11%)	9 (18%)	15 (14%)
Practical support[38]	2 (10%)	3 (8%)	8 (16%)	13 (12%)
Address attitudes/behaviour [39] associated with offending	2 (10%)	2 (5%)	8 (16%)	12 (11%)
Get through/monitor order[40]	2 (10%)	5 (14%)	5 (10%)	12 (11%)
Personal development[41]	5 (25%)	2 (5%)	2 (4%)	9 (8%)
Personal relationships[42]	-	2 (5%)	6 (12%)	8 (8%)
Other	2 (10%)	2 (5%)	2 (4%)	6 (6%)

The relative frequency of different types of objectives also differed according to the characteristics of probationers. Offending was more often identified as an objective in orders relating to young offenders (75 per cent compared with 34 per cent of adults) as were employment/education (40 per cent compared with 19 per cent) and accommodation (18 per cent compared with 11 per cent). Family relationships featured more commonly among the objectives for older offenders (23 per cent compared with 12 per cent of young offenders) as did alcohol abuse (38 per cent compared with 16 per cent). Amongst young offenders the most commonly identified objectives were offending (75 per cent), employment/education (40 per cent), drugs (25 per cent) and accommodation (18 per cent). Amongst adults they were alcohol abuse (38 per cent), offending (34 per cent), drugs (26 per cent) and family relationships (23 per cent).

Gender differences in respect of the objectives identified in probation case files were also apparent. Thus addressing offending behaviour featured more often as an objective among male probationers than females (64 per cent compared with 11 per cent) as did employment (35 per cent compared with 6 per cent) and drugs (27 per cent compared with 17 per cent). Providing help in relation to financial issues featured more commonly among female probationers (28 per cent compared with 12 per cent), as did practical help (22 per cent compared with 12 per cent), personal relationships (17 per cent compared with 5 per cent) and "personal development" (17 per cent compared with 8 per cent). The objectives most often identified for male probationers were offending (64 per cent), employment/education (35 per cent), drugs (27 per cent) and alcohol (25 per cent). Objectives related to alcohol use (33 per cent), financial problems (28 per cent) and the provision of practical support (22 per cent) were those most commonly identified for women.

In comparison with persistent offenders, first or early offenders more often were identified as having objectives related to financial problems (19 per cent compared with 9 per cent). Alcohol abuse, on the other hand, was more likely to feature among persistent offenders (30 per cent compared with 16 per cent) as were objectives related to the abuse of drugs (32 per cent compared with 19 per cent). Offending was more often an objective among "dishonesty" offenders than among "conduct" or "other" offenders (68 per cent compared with 41 per cent and 35 per cent). Drug-related objectives were least common among "conduct" offenders (15 per cent compared with 29 per cent of "dishonesty" offenders and 30 per cent of "other" offenders). Alcohol abuse was, on the other hand, more often an objective with "conduct" offenders than with the other two groups (41 per

---

[38] Settle lifestyle (8) child care (5) use of leisure (1) think about the future (1).
[39] Anger management/violence (10) peer group (3) destructiveness (1) racist attitudes (1).
[40] Monitor other conditions (7) monitor behaviour (3) get through special programme (1) monitor court appearances (1).
[41] Improve self-esteem (4) social skills (3) grow up (1) improve appearance (1) problem solving (1).
[42] Includes relationships with authority.

cent compared with 17 per cent and 30 per cent), as was the provision of practical support (26 per cent compared with 10 per cent of each of the other two groups) and addressing attitudes or behaviour associated with offending (26 per cent compared with 6 per cent and 20 per cent). The latter category consists in large part of intervention directed towards the management of violence or aggression.

Thirty per cent of objectives identified in case files were assessed as having been achieved completely; 29 per cent to a significant extent; 14 per cent partially; and 7 per cent to a limited extent. No progress had apparently been made towards the achievement of 21 per cent of objectives. All of the objectives in Burns were assessed as having been achieved either completely or to a significant extent. This was also true of 69 per cent of objectives in Bruce, 71 per cent in Scott and 43 per cent in Wallace. As we shall see in the following section, orders were more likely to have been breached in Wallace than in the other study areas which may account for the lower percentage of objectives which had been fully achieved or achieved to a significant degree. Only 14 per cent of objectives were achieved completely or to a significant extent in the case of breached offenders compared with 74 per cent of objectives in the case of offenders who completed their orders and 87 per cent in the case of those whose orders were discharged early on the grounds of satisfactory progress having been made. Indeed, when probationers who were breached were excluded from the analysis, the proportions of objectives achieved totally or to a significant degree were 68 per cent in Bruce, 85 per cent in Scott and 69 per cent in Wallace. If anything, it appears that social workers in Scott had made the greatest progress towards achieving the objectives associated with probation supervision.

The extent to which different types of objectives were assessed as having been achieved is summarised in Table 3.14. The greatest success appears to have been made in respect of providing probationers with practical support, addressing attitudes or behaviour supportive of offending and assisting their personal development, each of which were considered to have been achieved in whole or to a significant degree in 80 per cent of instances. The least progress appeared to have been made with respect to employment and accommodation. Offending related objectives were assessed as having been achieved totally or to a significant extent in 56 per cent of cases.

Table 3.14: The extent to which objectives were achieved[43]

	Number of objectives[44] achieved/total	Percentage of objectives achieved
Offending	34/61	56
Employment	11/33	33
Alcohol	18/29	62
Drugs	16/28	57
Family relationships	12/19	63
Accommodation	6/16	38
Financial	10/16	62
Practical support	12/15	80
Attitudes/behaviour associated with offending	12/15	80
Get through/monitor order	9/12	75
Personal development	8/10	80
Personal relationships	5/8	62
Other	4/7	57

A higher proportion of objectives were achieved completely or to a significant extent in the case of adult compared with young offenders (70 per cent compared with 49 per cent), women compared with men (83 per cent compared with 55 per cent), first or early compared with persistent offenders (70 per cent compared with 47 per cent) and "conduct" offenders compared with "dishonesty" offenders (64 per cent compared with 51 per cent). As with area differences, these differences can be accounted for to a considerable extent by the relative incidence of breaches in the various categories. When breaches were excluded from the analysis, the age difference largely disappeared (72 per cent and 80 per cent of objectives being achieved in the case of young and adult offenders) and the gender difference was reduced (74 per cent and 88 per cent of objectives

---

[43] The number and percentage of objectives achieved completely or to a significant extent.
[44] The column totals do not equate with the previous table since the objectives in Burns cases have been included here.

being achieved in the case of male and female probationers). Objectives were, however, still more likely to be achieved in the case of first or early offenders than persistent offenders (83 per cent compared with 68 per cent) and the proportion of objectives achieved with "dishonesty" and "conduct" offenders was reversed, with 78 per cent of objectives being achieved completely or to a significant extent in the former category and 69 per cent in the latter.

COMPLIANCE AND ENFORCEMENT

The National Standards stipulate that formal warnings should be issued to probationers for failure to comply with the requirements of their orders and that breach proceedings should be initiated in the event of non-compliance following a maximum of two formal warnings. Breach proceedings should also be instituted automatically in respect of probationers who are convicted of further offences committed while subject to supervision.

Across the sample as a whole 52 probationers (46 per cent) received at least one formal warning for non-compliance during their orders. One of the five probationers in Burns received one formal warning. The relevant data for the other research areas are summarised in Table 3.15 which indicates that the maximum number of formal warnings prior to breach proceedings being initiated as specified in the National Standards was exceeded in only four per cent of cases, all of which were in Wallace.

Table 3.15: Number of formal warnings by area

	Bruce	Scott	Wallace	Total
None	13 (65%)	23 (62%)	20 (40%)	56 (52%)
One	4 (20%)	5 (14%)	10 (20%)	19 (18%)
Two	3 (15%)	9 (24%)	16 (32%)	28 (26%)
Three	-	-	4 (8%)	4 (4%)
Total	20	37	50	107

Sixty per cent of probationers in Wallace received at least one formal warning, with 40 per cent receiving two or more. This compares with 35 per cent of probationers in Bruce and 38 per cent in Scott receiving one or more formal warnings. As Table 3.16 indicates, however, the more frequent issuing of warnings in Wallace was also accompanied by a significantly higher breach rate in that area. All five cases in Burns, which have been excluded from Table 3.16, were terminated on successful completion of the order. Probation orders were most likely to have been discharged early in Bruce reflecting, perhaps, the generally less serious criminal histories of probationers in that area. The high breach rate in Wallace, on the other hand, is consistent with the higher proportion of offenders with more serious criminal histories in the Wallace sample. As we saw in Chapter Two, there was a direct relationship between criminal history and the likelihood of a probation order being breached.

Table 3.16: Reason for termination of order by area

	Bruce	Scott	Wallace	Total
Early discharge	6 (30%)	5 (14%)	6 (12%)	17 (16%)
Completion	13 (65%)	23 (62%)	19 (38%)	55 (51%)
Breach	1 (5%)	9 (24%)	24 (48%)	34 (32%)
Death	-	-	1 (2%)	1 (1%)
Total	20	37	50	107

Across the sample as a whole, 32 per cent of cases resulted in the order being breached and the probationer re-sentenced for the original offence. The number of formal warnings issued varied according to the reason for termination of the order. No formal warnings had been issued in respect of 62 per cent of probationers who completed their probation orders in full and 76 per cent of those whose orders were discharged early by the courts. By contrast, only 26 per cent of offenders who were breached had no formal warnings recorded against them (in all cases these were probationers whose orders were breached as a consequence of further offending on probation): 21 per cent had received one formal warning; 47 per cent had received two; and six per cent had received a formal warning on three occasions.

A total of 38 offenders were returned to court for failure to comply with their probation orders or for having been convicted of a further offence. In seven cases the probation order was continued by the court. In three of these cases the offender was breached on a second occasion and the order subsequently revoked. In other words, there was a total of 41 breach applications relating to 38 probationers, with 34 orders terminated as a consequence of breach. In 15 instances - each relating to further offending by the probationer - breach proceedings were initiated without any formal warnings having been issued. In seven instances probationers were issued with one formal warning prior to breach, in 17 cases with two, and in two cases breach proceedings followed the issuing of three formal warnings by the social worker.

Nineteen breach applications resulted from the probationer's conviction for a further offence, 14 were a consequence of the offender's failure to report to the supervising social worker as instructed, seven were prompted by failure to comply with additional requirements and in one case the probationer had failed to inform the social worker of a change of address.

In nine cases the breach report recommended that the probation order be continued while in two others the social worker recommended that the probation order be strengthened by the attachment of additional requirements. Community service was recommended in two cases and a deferred sentence in one. In one case the social worker indicated in the breach report that a social work disposal was inappropriate while in 24 breach reports (58 per cent) no recommendation was made.

Twenty of the 34 offenders who were breached received a custodial sentence, four received community service orders and one was fined. Sentence was deferred in one case and the final outcome was unknown in four others. Two offenders had additional requirements - one residential and one to attend a special programme - attached to their existing orders.

Thirty-seven offenders (33 per cent of the sample) were recorded in files as having been convicted of (28 cases) or charged with (nine cases) a new offence while on probation. Twenty-five offenders had been charged or convicted on one occasion, seven had been convicted or charged twice and five had been convicted or charged three or more times. One offender in Burns and 25 per cent of probationers in Bruce and Scott had a new conviction or charge while subject to probation. In Wallace this was true of 22 probationers - 44 per cent of the sample in that area. The greater incidence of further offending in Wallace no doubt reflects the fact that the probation sample in this area contained a higher proportion of persistent offenders. What is of greater note is the comparable rates of new charges or convictions in Bruce and Scott, despite the fact that social workers in the latter area were dealing with higher proportions of offenders with more extensive criminal histories.

Information about the nature of offences was known in respect of 56 new convictions or charges. The main offence in the majority of cases (31) involved dishonesty - mainly housebreakings or thefts - while nine cases involved a breach of the peace and four a common assault. Four new charges or convictions related to non-sexual crimes of violence and four to road traffic offences. One probationer had been convicted of rape, another of possession of cannabis and two had been charged with breaches of court orders (a bail order and an interdict).

Eighty-four per cent of new offences involving dishonesty were committed or alleged to have been committed by probationers who had received their probation orders for offences of that type. Sixty-five per cent of convictions or charges in respect of probationers who had received their orders for dishonesty offences were for offences of a similar type, 22 per cent were for breaches of the peace or offences involving violence and 12 per cent were for other types of offence. Six of the ten new charges or convictions relating to offenders who received probation for breaches of public order or assaults were of a similar type (five breaches of the peace and one assault). Four of the new charges or convictions relating to probationers whose orders were imposed for other types of offences involved dishonesty and two were for serious assaults. Since information regarding new offences was obtained from social work files, accurate information concerning the date of the actual or alleged offence was sometimes not available and it is not therefore possible to comment further on the relative pattern and frequency of offending before and during probation supervision.

The court outcome was known in 43 cases (in 12 others the offender had not yet been convicted and in one other a warrant to apprehend had been issued by the court following the offender's failure to appear for sentence). Nineteen convictions resulted in the imposition of a custodial sentence and in ten other cases sentence was deferred. Six convictions resulted in the imposition of a community service order and in four cases new probation orders were imposed, two of which carried additional requirements to attend an intensive probation programme. Finally, two cases resulted in the offender being fined and in two others the offender was admonished.

SUMMARY AND CONCLUSIONS

Since the present study was concerned with assessing the effectiveness of probation supervision following the introduction of 100 per cent funding and National Standards, it was necessary to examine the extent to which significant benchmarks contained within the Standards were being achieved. The National Standard which stipulates that probationers should first be seen within one week of the order being made was met in 67 per cent of cases; the requirement of at least eight contacts in the first three months was met in 44 per cent of cases; that requiring at least two home visits in the first three months in 47 per cent of cases; and the timing of initial reviews in 51 per cent of cases. With the exception of home visits, the Standards were consistently less often met in Bruce than in the other study areas. The lower number of reviews in Wallace appeared to be attributable to the higher percentage of breached orders in that area.

Action plans were present in all but three probation case files. Offending behaviour, personal relationships and employment featured most often in action plans and in the services offered to probationers. The majority of services were delivered on an individual basis and most were provided by the supervising social worker. Other individuals or agencies were most likely to be involved in the provision of services relating to employment, alcohol, drugs and health issues. The objectives most often identified in case files focused upon offending, employment, alcohol and drugs. Around three-fifths of objectives appeared to have been achieved in full or to a significant degree though this was true of only 14 per cent of objectives identified in respect of probationers who were breached. Objectives relating to offending behaviour appeared to have been achieved completely or to a significant extent in 56 per cent of cases; those relating to employment or accommodation appeared least often to have been achieved. Objectives were less likely to have been achieved in Wallace (43 per cent) than in Bruce (69 per cent) or Scott (71 per cent), but this was attributable to the higher proportion of breaches in that area. With breaches excluded, objectives appeared more often to have been achieved in Scott (85 per cent) than in Bruce (68 per cent) or Wallace (69 per cent).

The highest breach rate and the highest proportion of probationers who received one or more formal warnings were found in Wallace, while probation orders in Bruce were more likely than in the other areas to have been terminated through an application for early discharge. Just under half the breach applications resulted from the probationer's conviction for a further offence and just over half of all breaches resulted in the imposition of a custodial sentence. Overall, just under a third of probationers were convicted of or charged with a further offence while on probation: the proportion was highest in Wallace and identical in Bruce and Scott, despite the fact that probationers in Scott might have been assumed, on the basis of their previous criminal histories, to present a higher risk of re-offending.

The areas of work identified in action plans, the services provided to probationers and the objectives of supervision varied across the research areas. Action plans in Bruce were less likely to include reference to offending behaviour, alcohol abuse or financial problems and were more likely to focus upon relationships and physical or mental health. Social workers in Bruce were more likely than those in the other areas to undertake work focused on relationships, the probationer's use of leisure time and physical or mental health. Offending featured less often as an objective of intervention while family relationships and the personal development of the probationer were more often objectives in Bruce than in Scott or Wallace.

In comparison with Bruce and Wallace, action plans in Scott placed less emphasis on employment. Services provided to probationers in Scott were more often addressed at offending behaviour, alcohol use, financial problems and social skills. The primary objectives in work with probationers in Scott appeared to relate to offending behaviour, drug abuse, alcohol abuse and financial problems.

Action plans in Wallace were least likely to include reference to the probationer's use of leisure time, and work undertaken with probationers in this area was less likely to focus upon accommodation, employment and drugs. The primary objectives in work with probationers in Wallace were broadly similar to those in Scott, focusing, in descending order of frequency, on offending, employment, alcohol and drugs. The apparent mismatch between probation objectives and services provided in Wallace is likely to be attributable to the high breach rate in that area which effectively prevented much work from being undertaken in a significant proportion of cases.

The argument initially developed in the concluding section of the previous chapter - that social workers in Bruce were adopting more of a welfare approach to probation supervision - is further reinforced, therefore, by the findings in the present chapter. Offending behaviour featured less often in Bruce in probation action plans, in the services provided to probationers and in the objectives of probation. By contrast, social workers in Bruce placed greater emphasis upon personal relationships in plans and in the process and objectives of supervision. In this respect social work practice in Bruce was least consistent with the principles and objectives of probation supervision as detailed in the National Standards. It was also, as we have already seen in this chapter, least likely to meet a range of standards which provide the framework for probation supervision in Scotland. Action plans, services provided and objectives pursued in Scott and Wallace, on the other hand, appeared more consistently to be directed towards addressing offending behaviour and other problems which might be assumed to contribute directly or indirectly to that behaviour. In Scott, where work was recorded more systematically and was subject to greater scrutiny by managers, probation objectives appeared more often to have been wholly or significantly achieved and a lower incidence of actual or alleged re-offending was observed than would have been expected in view of the characteristics of probationers in that area.

Probation packages also varied, however, according to the characteristics of individual offenders. Offending, employment and accommodation featured more often in the action plans of young offenders and in the objectives pursued, while offending and employment provided a focus for intervention more often with young offenders than with adults. Alcohol abuse, medical or mental health problems and violence were more often identified in the action plans of adult offenders, services to adult offenders were more likely to focus upon these issues and upon relationships, and probation objectives for adult offenders were more likely to relate to alcohol abuse and family relationships. Probation objectives were more often achieved in full or to a significant extent with adult offenders, though much of this difference could be accounted for by the higher proportion of young offenders who were breached.

Action plans in respect of first or early offenders were more likely than those developed in respect of persistent offenders to contain reference to relationships and accommodation. Services provided to this category of probationer more often focused upon relationships, financial issues, the probationer's use of leisure time and offending, while addressing financial problems was more often an objective of supervision than with persistent offenders. The action plans of persistent offenders and the services provided more often focused upon alcohol and drug abuse and violence, and objectives related to the abuse of alcohol or drugs featured more prominently with this category of offender. The greater apparent focus by supervising social workers upon offending behaviour with first or early offenders may reflect the higher breach rate among persistent offenders and the higher proportion of the latter who attended intensive probation projects aimed at tackling offending behaviour. Probation objectives were more likely to be achieved with first or early offenders than with persistent offenders even when "successful" orders alone were considered. This may be a reflection of the chaotic lifestyles of many persistent offenders, more entrenched attitudes and behaviour and more deeply rooted personal problems such as those relating to the abuse of drugs.

Offending and employment were more often identified in the action plans of probationers who had received their orders for main offences involving dishonesty, and probation supervision was more likely with this group of probationers to focus on financial issues. Addressing offending and drug abuse featured more often in the objectives pursued. By comparison, alcohol abuse, medical or mental health problems and violence featured more prominently in the action plans of offenders convicted of violent offences or offences against public order and these issues, in addition to relationships, were more often identified as a focus for intervention. Addressing alcohol abuse, providing the offender with practical support and addressing attitudes or behaviour supportive of offending (in most instances relating to violence or aggression) were more often objectives of supervision with this group of offenders. When successful orders alone were considered, objectives were more often achieved in whole or to a significant degree in respect of probationers sentenced for offences involving dishonesty.

Turning finally to gender differences, offending behaviour, alcohol and drug abuse, employment and use of leisure time were more often included in the action plans of male probationers. Offending, employment and drug abuse were more likely in the case of male probationers to feature as objectives of supervision and as a focus for service provision. Women's action plans, on the other hand, more often contained reference to accommodation, education and financial problems, and work undertaken with female probationers more often focused upon accommodation, financial issues, medical or mental health problems, social skills, violence and child care. Addressing financial problems, providing practical support, improving personal relationships and focusing upon the personal development of the probationer were more often identified as objectives with female offenders. Objectives were more often achieved with female probationers, this difference being accounted for partly, but not entirely, by the lower breach rate among women.

Just as the explanations of offending and the reasons for recommending probation varied according to the characteristics of individual offenders, so too, clearly, did the packages of supervision provided, the objectives pursued and the extent to which they were achieved. In the following chapter these issues are further explored through an examination of social workers' perceptions of the effectiveness of supervision in individual cases and, in particular, the extent to which it was considered to have impacted upon the risk of further offending by the probationer.

CHAPTER FOUR

SOCIAL WORKERS' VIEWS OF THE EFFECTIVENESS OF SUPERVISION

INTRODUCTION

Supervising social workers were invited, in respect of each of the cases included in the main study sample, to complete a brief questionnaire following the termination of the probation order. The questionnaire, which consisted of a mixture of fixed choice and open ended questions, sought to elicit their views as to the effectiveness of probation in individual cases. Specific areas addressed in the questionnaire included the social workers and probationer's definitions of the main issues in the case; objectives of supervision and the extent to which they were achieved; the probationer's response to supervision and what they found most and least helpful about probation; and social workers' perceptions of the risk of continued offending and, where relevant, the contribution of probation in reducing that risk.

Ninety-six completed questionnaires were returned from a total possible sample of 112 and related to 51 young offenders (aged between 16 and 20 years when made subject to probation) and 45 adults (aged 21 years and over). The present chapter describes the findings from this element of the study which reflect social workers' perceptions of the effectiveness of probation supervision.

SOCIAL WORKERS' AND PROBATIONERS' DEFINITIONS OF ISSUES

Social workers were invited to identify what they perceived to have been the main issues in the case and what they believed their probationer had considered the main issues to have been. In both instances up to four separate issues could be identified. Consistent with previous research (Duffee and Clark, 1985)[45] social workers tended to identify more issues in a case than did their probationers (Table 4.1). For instance, while three or four main issues were defined by social workers in 78 cases, a similar number of issues were believed by social workers to have been identified by only 55 probationers.

Table 4.1: Social workers' views as to the number of issues identified by them and by their probationers

Number of issues	Social Workers	Probationers
Four	51 (53%)	31 (33%)
Three	27 (28%)	24 (25%)
Two	15 (16%)	26 (27%)
One	3 (3%)	13 (14%)
Nil	0	2 (2%)
Total	96	96

The social workers' views of the main issues in each case and their perceptions of their probationers' views are summarised in Table 4.2. It should be noted that in this, and in several other tables in this chapter, since more than one issue was identified in the majority of cases the column total exceeds the number of cases involved.

It is evident from Table 4.2 that, with the exception of accommodation, employment and child care (which were viewed by similar numbers of social workers and probationers as being relevant issues in a case) and financial issues and the avoidance of a custodial sentence (upon which greater emphasis was thought to be placed by probationers than by social workers), most other areas were more often thought to be perceived by social workers than by probationers as issues requiring attention.

Social workers, in particular, were considerably more likely to have identified offending behaviour, drug use and peer group influences as among the main issues in a case and somewhat more likely than probationers to

---

[45] Duffee, D.E. and Clark, D. (1985) The frequency and classification of the needs of offenders in community settings, *Journal of Criminal Justice*, 13, 243-68

have focused upon the need for emotional support, aggression or violence, lack of self esteem, alcohol abuse family relationships and use of leisure time as areas worthy of attention. To the extent that social workers placed greater emphasis than did probationers upon social and emotional needs, these findings are consistent with the review undertaken by Duffee and Clark (1985) of studies which had sought to identify the needs of offenders in community settings.

Table 4.2: Social workers' views as to the main issues identified by themselves and the probationer

Issue	Identified by social worker (n=96)	Identified by probationer (n=96)
Offending	56 (58%)	40 (42%)
Drug use	40 (42%)	25 (26%)
Employment/education	32 (33%)	32 (33%)
Accommodation	28 (29%)	28 (29%)
Alcohol use	24 (25%)	19 (20%)
Family relationships	19 (20%)	14 (15%)
Peer group influences	17 (18%)	7 (7%)
Personal relationships	12 (12%)	10 (10%)
Aggression/violence	12 (12%)	5 (5%)
Emotional support	12 (12%)	6 (6%)
Lack of self esteem	11 (11%)	5 (5%)
Child care	9 (9%)	9 (9%)
Financial	9 (9%)	19 (20%)
Use of leisure time	7 (7%)	2 (2%)
Attitudes supportive of offending	6 (6%)	4 (4%)
Physical/mental health	5 (5%)	2 (2%)
Stabilise lifestyle	5 (5%)	4 (4%)
General/practical support	5 (5%)	5 (5%)
Monitor other conditions/orders	4 (4%)	6 (6%)
Social/personal skills	3 (3%)	1 (1%)
Monitor behaviour/get through order	2 (2%)	6 (6%)
Avoid custody	0 (0%)	12 (13%)

PROBATION OBJECTIVES AND THEIR ACHIEVEMENT

Offending behaviour was viewed by social workers as being one of the main issues in 58 per cent of probation cases. This may seem, on the face of it, to be a surprisingly low figure given that probation is generally agreed to be a vehicle for addressing offending behaviour. The results presented in Table 4.2 would suggest, instead, that although their probationers were placed on probation as a consequence of having offended, in some instances social workers believed that other social and personal problems needed to be addressed, either before the offending behaviour could be tackled directly or as a means in itself to impacting positively upon the risk of continued offending. Such a suggestion is consistent with the finding, presented in Table 4.3, that addressing offending or preventing offending featured as an explicit objective in 77 per cent of cases.

Table 4.3 summarises the main objectives identified by social workers for each of the 96 cases in the sample and the extent to which they were perceived by social workers to have been achieved. For the sake of consistency, the same categories employed in the previous chapter have been adopted. The composition of the categories can be found in the footnotes on page 32.

Table 4.3: Objectives and the extent to which they were perceived to have been achieved

Objective	Number of cases	Percentage of cases (n=96)	Percentage of cases in which objective was achieved[46]
Offending	74	77%	44/74 (60%)
Drugs	34	35%	13/34 (38%)
Practical support	29	30%	10/29 (41%)
Get through/monitor order	25	26%	14/25 (56%)
Attitudes/behaviour associated with offending	24	25%	8/24 (33%)
Employment/education	23	24%	11/23 (48%)
Alcohol	21	22%	7/21 (33%)
Accommodation	21	22%	10/21 (48%)
Personal development	14	15%	6/14 (43%)
Family relationships	13	14%	6/13 (46%)
Personal relationships	9	9%	6/9 (67%)
Financial	7	7%	2/7 (29%)
Other	7	7%	3/7 (43%)

There were some area differences in the objectives reported by social workers, though they were less marked than in the previous chapter. Practical support was more often an objective in Scott (40 per cent) and Bruce (33 per cent) than in Wallace (19 per cent). Drug abuse featured more often in Scott (40 per cent) than in Wallace (31 per cent) or Bruce (33 per cent). Employment related objectives were more common in Wallace than in Bruce or Scott (29 per cent compared with 19 per cent and 20 per cent) as were objectives concerning family relationships (19 per cent compared with 9 per cent and 10 per cent) and personal relationships (24 per cent compared with 5 per cent in Bruce and no cases in Scott). Finally, alcohol abuse was more often mentioned in Scott (27 per cent) than in Wallace (21 per cent) or Bruce (14 per cent). Offending behaviour featured as an objective in 76 per cent of cases in Bruce, 77 per cent in Scott and 79 per cent in Wallace.

Comparison of these findings with the data presented in Table 3.13 reveals some differences which deserve further comment. In particular, offending behaviour appeared to feature as an explicit objective in only 25 per cent of case files in Bruce but was mentioned by social workers as being an objective in 76 per cent of cases. Conversely, analysis of the case files in Bruce suggested that work on family relationships was an objective in 30 per cent of cases, but according to social workers this was an objective of supervision in only nine per cent of cases. Had the argument presented in previous chapters - that social workers in Bruce tended to adopt a welfare model of probation supervision - been based only upon analysis of objectives in case files, the present results would appear to contradict that assumption. However, addressing offending behaviour featured less often in the reasons for recommending probation in Bruce, in probation action plans and in the analysis of social work services provided. The present finding, therefore, may suggest that addressing offending was often an **implicit** objective in Bruce, less often to be addressed directly and more often to be addressed indirectly through the amelioration of other problems. Such an explanation is consistent with the argument previously advanced and would reconcile the apparently contradictory findings which have emerged.

Offending featured more often as an objective among young offenders than adults (82 per cent compared with 71 per cent). Alcohol abuse was more often an objective for adult offenders (36 per cent compared with 12 per cent) as was providing help with family relationships (18 per cent compared with 10 per cent). Addressing offending was more often identified as an objective with male probationers than with females (81 per cent compared with 56 per cent). Other objectives more commonly identified for men than for women were drugs (39 per cent compared with 12 per cent), alcohol (25 per cent compared with 12 per cent) and getting the probationer through or monitoring the order (28 per cent compared with 19 per cent). Providing practical help or support was, on the other hand, an objective more often attributed to probation practice with women (56 per cent compared with 25 per cent). Providing help with financial problems was an objective with 25 per cent

---

[46] Objective achieved completely or to a significant extent.

of female probationers and 4 per cent of males; similarly, objectives related to personal development of the probationer were more often identified for female than for male offenders (38 per cent compared with 10 per cent) as were those which focused upon attitudes or behaviour associated with offending (38 per cent compared with 22 per cent).

Addressing offending behaviour was equally likely to be an objective with first or early offenders and with persistent offenders, being identified in 79 and 78 per cent of cases respectively. Work with first or early offenders was, however, more likely to focus on material problems. Thus employment was more often an objective with this category of probationer (34 per cent compared with 13 per cent) as were accommodation (24 per cent compared with 13 per cent) and financial issues (14 per cent compared with 4 per cent). Work with persistent offenders more often focused upon offering support of a practical nature (35 per cent compared with 24 per cent), drugs (39 per cent compared with 24 per cent), alcohol (28 per cent compared with 7 per cent) and personal relationships (17 per cent compared with 3 per cent).

Turning, finally, to the main offences in respect of which the probation order had been made, offending behaviour was more often identified as an objective with "dishonesty" offenders (83 per cent compared with 64 per cent of "conduct" offenders and 76 per cent of "other" offenders) as was getting the probationer through or monitoring the order (31 per cent compared with 24 per cent and 12 per cent). Addressing alcohol abuse was most common among "conduct" offenders (40 per cent compared with 15 per cent of "dishonesty" offenders and 24 per cent of "other" offenders) as was addressing attitudes or behaviour associated with offending (44 per cent compared with 13 per cent and 35 per cent).

The areas in which the greatest progress had been made in terms of objectives being achieved (that is, objectives had been totally achieved or achieved to a significant extent in more than half the relevant cases) were: personal relationships, addressing or avoiding offending[47], and getting through/monitoring the order. Objectives which were least likely to have been achieved (that is, were achieved totally or to a significant extent in fewer than 40 per cent of relevant cases) included: financial problems, alcohol abuse, addressing attitudes associated with offending and drug abuse. The relative lack of importance apparently attached by social workers to financial problems may, therefore, represent a realistic assessment on their part of their inability to impact significantly upon the poverty experienced by many probationers (Stewart and Stewart, 1993[48]; Stewart et al., 1994). On the other hand, the limited progress made in addressing violence or aggression, alcohol and drug abuse may reflect the deep rooted nature of these problems and/or the limited effectiveness of individual intervention in successfully addressing issues of this kind. What is more encouraging is the relative success that social workers met with in addressing some of the more common social problems facing offenders - such as employment and accommodation - though, as we shall see later, social workers were often reluctant to take credit for some of the material improvements in their probationers' lives.

In Bruce, 76 per cent of objectives were believed to have been achieved, compared with 43 per cent in Scott and 34 per cent in Wallace. When breaches were excluded, 76 per cent, 55 per cent and 51 per cent of objectives were thought by social workers to have been achieved completely or to a significant extent in these three study areas. As in Chapter Three, objectives were more often believed to have been achieved in respect of first or early offenders compared with persistent offenders (65 per cent compared with 37 per cent) and in respect of women compared with men (56 per cent compared with 44 per cent). When breaches were excluded the gender difference disappeared, but objectives were still less likely to have been achieved with persistent offenders (53 per cent) than with first or early offenders (73 per cent).

PROBATIONERS' RESPONSES TO SUPERVISION

Motivation to Address Problems

Social workers were asked to rate their probationers according to how motivated they were to address their offending behaviour and to address other problems. Thirty-two per cent of probationers were believed to have been highly motivated to address their offending, 51 per cent were said to have been fairly motivated and 17 per cent had shown no motivation to do so. Twenty-seven per cent were said to have been very motivated to address other problems, 54 per cent fairly motivated and 19 per cent not at all motivated to do so. There was a clear association between motivation to address offending and motivation to address other problems: probationers who were highly motivated to address their offending were most likely to be highly motivated to

---

[47] Addressing offending may or may not imply an expectation that a total cessation of offending can be achieved within the currency of an order; avoiding offending, on the other hand, suggests that prevention of offending during the order was considered to be an objective in the case. The former term implies progression to an eventual goal while the latter reflects a hope that probation may, in the very least, have a 'holding effect' in relation to further offending behaviour.

[48] Stewart, G & Stewart, J. (1993) *Social Circumstances of younger offenders under supervision*, London: Association of Chief Officers of Probation.

address other issues; whilst those who were least motivated to deal with their offending behaviour were also least motivated to address other problems.

Probationers in Wallace were less often described by their supervising social workers as having been very motivated to address their offending (17 per cent compared with 48 per cent in Bruce and 40 per cent in Scott) or other problems (14 per cent compared with 38 per cent and 37 per cent). Wallace probationers were most likely to have shown no motivation to address their offending (24 per cent compared with 5 per cent in Bruce and 17 per cent in Scott) or to address other problems (29 per cent compared with 5 per cent and 17 per cent).

There was, however, a clear association between the reasons for probation orders being terminated and offenders' motivation to address offending and other issues. Motivation was highest, as might be expected, among probationers whose orders were discharged early and lowest among those whose orders were revoked as a consequence of breach[49]. Probationers in Wallace were least likely to complete their period of probation supervision. Even when breaches were excluded, however, Wallace probationers were still less often considered to have been highly motivated to address their offending (24 per cent compared with 50 per cent in Bruce and 57 per cent in Scott) or to address other problems (19 per cent compared with 35 per cent and 52 per cent).

Table 4.4: Motivation to address offending and reason for termination of order

How motivated	Early discharge		Completion		Breach	
Very	11	(69%)	18	(37%)	2	(7%)
Fairly	5	(31%)	27	(55%)	17	(57%)
Not at all	0		4	(8%)	11	(37%)
Total	16		49		30	

Table 4.5: Motivation to address other problems and reason for termination of order

How motivated	Early discharge		Completion		Breach	
Very	9	(56%)	14	(29%)	3	(10%)
Fairly	7	(43%)	30	(61%)	15	(50%)
Not at all	0		5	(10%)	12	(40%)
Total	16		49		30	

There was also a relationship between motivation and age. Young offenders were slightly less likely than older probationers to be assessed by their social workers as having been very motivated to address their offending and other problems. Twenty-seven percent of the young offenders were classified as very motivated to address their offending compared with 38 per cent of adult probationers. Similarly, while 22 per cent of young probationers were described as highly motivated to address other problems, this was said to be true of 33 per cent of adults.

Female probationers were more likely than males to have been described as highly motivated to address their offending (44 per cent compared with 30 per cent) and other problems (38 per cent compared with 25 per cent). First or early offenders were more likely than persistent offenders to have been perceived as very motivated to address both their offending (52 per cent compared with 26 per cent) and other issues (41 per cent compared with 24 per cent). "Dishonesty" offenders were more likely than "conduct" or "other" offenders to have shown no motivation to address their offending behaviour (22 per cent compared with 8 per cent and 12 per cent).

With breaches excluded from the analysis, young offenders and older probationers were equally likely to have been highly motivated to address their offending (43 per cent compared with 46 per cent) but the latter were more often said to be highly motivated to address other issues (40 per cent compared with 29 per cent). The gender difference disappeared but persistent offenders were still less likely to have been considered highly motivated to address their offending than first or early offenders (42 per cent compared with 61 per cent), though the two groups did not differ to any significant degree in their motivation to address other problems (38 per cent compared with 44 per cent). "Dishonesty" offenders were now more often said to be highly motivated to address their offending (57 per cent) than either "conduct" (38 per cent) or "other" (29 per cent) probationers.

---

49 Tables 4.4 and 4.5 exclude one probationer who died prior to expiry of his order.

Response to Supervision

Social workers were also asked to categorise their probationer's overall response to supervision. Twenty-nine per cent of probationers were believed to have shown a very positive response to probation and 32 per cent were said to have shown a fairly positive response. In 24 per cent of cases the probationer's response was described as mixed and in 15 per cent as fairly (5 per cent) or very (10 per cent) poor.

Just as probationers' motivation to address their offending and other issues in the context of probation supervision varied according to the eventual outcome of the order, so too did their overall response to probation. The most consistently positive responses to supervision were found among those whose orders had been discharged early (this not being surprising since an application for early discharge is prompted by a probationer having made significant and sufficient progress during the course of supervision) while probationers who were breached were most likely to have been described as demonstrating a mixed or poor response to their orders (Table 4.6).

Table 4.6: Response to supervision as assessed by the social worker and reason for termination of order[50]

Response to supervision	Early discharge	Completion	Breach
Very positive	9 (56%)	17 (35%)	2 (7%)
Fairly positive	7 (44%)	20 (41%)	4 (13%)
Mixed	0	10 (20%)	13 (43%)
Poor	0	2 (4 %)	11 (37%)
Total	16	49	30

Probationers in Bruce were more often said to have shown a very positive or fairly positive response to probation supervision (81 per cent compared with 66 per cent in Scott and 45 per cent in Wallace). This difference appears, however, to reflect to a significant extent the different proportions of orders which were breached in the three study areas. When breaches were excluded from the analysis, 88 per cent of probationers in Bruce, 86 per cent in Scott and 72 per cent in Wallace were believed to have responded positively to probation supervision.

There was also a clear association between an offender's response to probation supervision and age. Thus while 51 per cent of young offenders were described as having responded positively to probation, this was true of 73 per cent of probationers aged 21 years or older. This age difference persisted, though was less marked, when only probationers who had completed their probation orders (in full or with an early discharge) were considered: 75 per cent of young offenders and 86 per cent of adults were now said to have shown a positive response to probation.

Women were more likely than men (75 per cent compared with 59 per cent) to have responded positively to probation and first or early offenders were more likely than persistent offenders (72 per cent compared with 58 per cent) to have shown a positive response. These differences disappeared, however, when probationers who were breached were excluded from the analysis.

Finally, "dishonesty" offenders were less often described as having responded positively to probation (56 per cent) than either "conduct" offenders (64 per cent) or "other" offenders (76 per cent). With breaches excluded, however, "conduct" offenders were somewhat less likely than "dishonesty" or "other" offenders to have shown a positive response (72 per cent compared with 87 per cent and 86 per cent).

Factors Affecting Probationer's Response

Social workers were asked to identify factors which they believed had affected their probationer's response to probation. Factors identified as having adversely affected the probationer's response are summarised in Table 4.7. They fell in the main into four broad headings: the existence of other social or personal problems which detracted from the probationer's willingness or ability to engage or comply (continued drug or alcohol abuse, personal/practical problems); personal characteristics which undermined the possibility of a more positive response (lack of self esteem, immaturity, resented being challenged); the influence or lack of support of significant others (lack of family support, peer relationships); and the probationer's lack of interest in the probation order (lack of interest, did not see relevance of probation).

---

[50] Excludes one probationer who died prior to expiry of his order.

Table 4.7: Social workers' views of the factors adversely affecting the probationer's response

	Number of cases (n=36)
Continued drug or alcohol abuse	8
Lack of interest	6
Personal/practical problems	5
Lack of self esteem	5
Immaturity	5
Lack of family support	3
Did not see relevance of probation	2
Peer relationships	2
Resented being challenged	1

Two other factors - employment and family responsibilities - were viewed in different cases as having affected the probationer's response in different ways. In two cases, for example, the fact that the probationers had obtained employment was viewed as having had a positive impact on their responses whilst in a third case the demands of employment had adversely affected the probationer's commitment to his probation order. Similarly, having family responsibilities was believed to have served to motivate two probationers but to have impacted negatively upon the responses of two others, in one case through a lack of child care provision.

Factors which were regarded as having consistently influenced probationers' responses in a positive way are summarised in Table 4.8. In most instances probationers were believed to have been motivated by their desire to avoid further offending and its likely consequences or breach (desire to avoid custody/breach, fear of consequences of further offending, motivated to stop offending) or their desire to obtain help with various problems in their lives (motivated to address problems). Features of probation supervision itself - the help received (valued input received on order), the relationship established with the social worker or the structure provided by the order (regular contact with social worker, clear about expectations) - also appeared in a sizable number of cases to have contributed to the probationer's positive response.

Table 4.8: Social workers' views of factors positively influencing responses to probation

	Number of cases (n=70)
Motivated to address problems	20
Valued input received on order	19
Desire to avoid custody/breach	19
Fear of consequences of further offending	13
Motivated to stop offending	9
Relationship with social worker	6
Insight into own behaviour	5
Regular contact with social worker	5
Clear about expectations	4
Supportive personal relationships	2
Annoyance at self	2

Turning now to what offenders were believed to have found most helpful about probation, the relevant responses are summarised in Table 4.9. Having someone to discuss their problems with and making progress in addressing their problems featured significantly in the factors advanced by social workers in this respect. The provision of practical support - which included referral to other agencies, liaison with other agencies and advocacy on behalf of probationers - was also considered to have been valued by a significant number of probationers. In eight cases social workers made reference to probationers having appreciated what has been described as "personal recognition": this included receiving praise and encouragement (five cases) and receiving attention (three cases). In seven cases explicit reference was made to the value probationers attached to the framework or structure offered by probation: the structure or rules associated with the probation order was mentioned in five cases while regular contact with the supervising officer was cited in another two. Finally, the role of the social worker was believed to have been found helpful in four cases, in three because of the objectivity of the social worker and in one as a result of the positive relationship established between social worker and probationer.

Table 4.9: Social workers' views of what their probationers found most helpful about probation

	Number of cases (n=80)
Having someone to discuss problems with	21
Practical support	18
Making progress in addressing problems	16
General support	12
Avoiding custody	8
Personal recognition	8
Framework/structure	7
Groupwork	5
Reminder to avoid offending	4
Role of the social worker	4
Nothing	8

Those aspects of probation which offenders were believed to have found least helpful are summarised in Table 4.10. Reference was made most frequently to factors associated with the appointments themselves - their rigidity, frequency or location (usually office based). In eight cases offenders had resented having their behaviour challenged or had been resistant to examining their own behaviour while in five cases the intrusiveness of probation - evidenced, for example, through the "social worker monitoring unsuitable relationships" or the "intrusion into family life" - was alluded to. Specific areas of work addressed during probation (such as violence and relaxation techniques) were referred to in four cases while in three others probationers were said to have no longer seen the relevance of probation once particular issues had been addressed and resolved. Finally, three probationers were thought not to have found reviews to be a helpful aspect of the probation process.

Table 4.10: Social workers' views of what their probationers found least helpful about probation

	Number of cases (n=59)
Nature of appointments	22
Having behaviour challenged	8
Intrusiveness	5
Specific areas of work	4
The need to continue on order	3
Reviews	3
Being on probation in the first place	3
Nothing	8

THE IMPACT OF PROBATION ON THE RISK OF RECIDIVISM

The final items in the social workers' questionnaires sought to elicit their views as to the risk of further offending presented by the probationer, whether that risk had changed since the offender had been placed on probation and, if it had reduced, the extent to which social work intervention as opposed to other factors had contributed to the perceived reduction in risk. Findings presented in this section relate to a total of 94 cases: in one case the probation order had been closed following the death of the probationer and in another the social worker was unable to offer an assessment of risk.

Risk of further offending

Forty per cent of probationers were considered unlikely to re-offend, 43 per cent were thought fairly likely to re-offend and 17 per cent were believed very likely to do so. Forty-eight per cent of probationers in Bruce were considered unlikely to re-offend compared with 43 per cent in Scott and 32 per cent in Wallace. None of the probationers in Bruce was considered by their social workers to have a very high risk of further offending, while this was true of 23 per cent in Scott and 22 per cent in Wallace. The area difference disappeared when breaches were excluded, however, with 50 per cent of Bruce and Wallace probationers and 57 per cent of Scott probationers being considered unlikely to re-offend.

The perceived risk of further offending was found to be related to a number of factors including probationers' willingness to address their offending and other problems, their response to probation and the reason for their order being terminated. There was a clear association between the social worker's assessment of risk and the extent to which offending related objectives were achieved. In 55 per cent of cases in which the objective of addressing offending had been achieved (either completely or to a significant extent) the probationer was considered unlikely to re-offend and in only two per cent of these cases was further offending thought very likely. By contrast, only seven per cent of probationers for whom offending-related objectives had been achieved only partially, to a limited extent or not at all were believed to be unlikely to re-offend, while in 39 per cent of these cases re-offending was considered very likely.

Perceived risk of re-offending was also related to age. More specifically, young offenders were more often considered to present a high risk of continued offending than were adults: 26 per cent of young offenders were thought very likely to re-offend compared with only seven per cent of adults. Even with breaches excluded this age difference persisted, with no adult offenders being considered very likely to re-offend compared with 18 per cent of probationers under 21 years of age. The question arises, of course, as to whether young offenders were more likely to be assessed as presenting a higher risk of continued offending simply by virtue of their age. Whilst age is one indicator which social workers may have taken into consideration when contemplating the risk presented by individual probationers, it is clear from the material presented later in this chapter that a wide range of indices were drawn upon in the construction of their responses.

Women were more likely than men to be considered unlikely to re-offend (56 per cent compared with 37 per cent) and fewer women than men were considered very likely to re-offend (6 per cent compared with 19 per cent). This gender difference appears, however, to be attributable to the differing characteristics of male and female probationers, such as to suggest that the former would present a greater risk of recidivism.

Previous criminal history is one clear indicator of future risk. Sixty-eight per cent of first or early offenders were thought unlikely to re-offend compared with only 27 per cent of persistent offenders. Even when "successful" probation orders alone were considered (that is, breaches were excluded) persistent offenders were more likely than first or early offenders to be considered at risk of re-offending (61 per cent compared with 23 per cent). Finally, "dishonesty" offenders were thought more often than "conduct" offenders or "other" offenders to present a very high risk of further offending (23 per cent compared with 8 per cent and 12 per cent).

In most instances social workers provided additional explanations for their assessment of risk in individual cases. These are summarised separately for "very likely" and "fairly likely" cases in Table 4.11. Reference was made in proportionately more cases of offenders considered very likely to re-offend to the fact that their attitudes were unchanged, they had continued to offend since they were placed on probation or they were, more generally, deeply entrenched in a pattern of offending behaviour.

> "The probationer was currently too enmeshed in pattern of behaviour with little insight or motivation to change."

> "He re-offended within a month of being placed on his second order and paid no heed to anyone."

> "Nothing has changed. Still no money, support, employment or motivation to stop offending. Still misusing substances."

A significant feature which appeared to distinguish between offenders assessed as very likely to re-offend and those deemed fairly likely to re-offend was the greater emphasis placed in relation to the latter group on potential circumstances or pressures which might result in further offending behaviour.

"[The probationer] is now living in an area of high delinquency where drugs are readily available should he so wish."

"I feel that [the probationer] is still liable to react to stressful or anxiety provoking situations by losing his self control which makes offending more possible."

"It will depend on the extent to which he can remain in employment/out of debt and if he can avoid being talked into alcohol/drug misuse by his 'friends'."

Table 4.11: Reasons provided by social workers for continued risk of offending

	Very likely (n=15)	Fairly likely (n=41)
Attitudes unchanged	9	10
Peer group influence	4	8
Circumstances unchanged or deteriorated	4	11
Continued offending	4	4
Enmeshed in pattern of offending	3	1
Continued drug use	2	3
May resort to further drug use	0	8
May resort to further alcohol abuse	0	7
May respond to external (environmental) pressures	0	7
May react under stress	0	6
Mental health problems	0	3
Other	0	2

In contrast, when commenting upon the reasons for considering probationers unlikely to re-offend, social workers drew upon a range of positive indices which are summarised in Table 4.12. Their responses could, broadly speaking, be grouped into three more general categories: those directly related to offending (has not re-offended, appears determined to stop offending, no extensive history of offending, factors relating to offending no longer an issue, positive response to probation and fears consequences of further offending); those related to improvements or stability in personal circumstances (in employment, stable circumstances, personal relationships and responsibilities, and control over use of alcohol or drugs); and those related to the acquisition of personal skills (better able to cope, has insight into behaviour and increased maturity).

"This individual did not have an extensive list of previous convictions to begin with. But she also really enjoyed probation and at the end review gave a clear commitment to avoiding crime."

"He has now 'grown away' from his mates and has a steady girlfriend who seems to be a good influence and of whom his mother approves. [The probationer] was placed on probation when he was 16, is now 19 and seems to be maturing in the right direction!"

"Offence was first and only and influenced by (now ended) friendship with a then chaotic drug using offender. Client is now fully given to responsible parenting and a stable home life."

"Offending behaviour almost totally related to past drug use. Given the level of control attained with regards to drugs, re-offending very unlikely."

"[The probationer] was homeless, had no income and was easily motivated to take and drive away cars. He now has a stable home, works in a garage and knows that another offence will mean jail."

Table 4.12: Reasons provided by social workers for being considered unlikely to re-offend

	(n=39)
In employment	10
Has not re-offended	8
Stable personal circumstances	8
Personal relationships or responsibilities	7
Appears determined to stop offending	6
No extensive history of offending	5
Factors related to offending no longer an issue	5
Better able to cope	4
Positive response to probation	4
No longer using drugs	3
Fears consequences of further offending	3
Has insight into behaviour	2
Has matured	2
Alcohol abuse has decreased	2

Changes in risk of re-offending

In addition to assessing the current risk of re-offending, social workers were asked to indicate whether that risk had changed since the offender was placed on probation. Seventy-three per cent of probationers were considered much less likely (31 per cent) or slightly less likely (42 per cent) to re-offend since being placed on probation. In 24 per cent of cases the risk of re-offending was thought to have remained unchanged. Only three probationers (three per cent) were thought more at risk of re-offending since being placed on probation. Ninety-five per cent of probationers in Bruce, 60 per cent in Scott and 67 per cent in Wallace were thought less likely to re-offend since being placed on probation. With breaches excluded the relevant figures were 95 per cent, 76 per cent and 75 per cent respectively.

Reductions in risk were most likely to occur among offenders who had been motivated to address their offending and other problems and amongst those who had responded most positively to probation supervision. Furthermore, probationers whose orders were discharged early were most likely to have been perceived as demonstrating a significant reduction in risk while those who were breached were least likely to be considered at less risk of offending compared with when they were placed on probation. Eighty-six per cent of probationers whose offending related objectives had been achieved completely or to a significant extent were thought less likely to re-offend compared with only 57 per cent of those whose offending related objectives were achieved partially, to a limited extent or not at all.

There was some evidence of an association between reduction in risk and age: while 80 per cent of adults were considered less at risk of offending since being made subject to probation this was true of only 66 per cent of offenders under 21 years of age. With breaches excluded, young offenders were still thought less often to have demonstrated a reduction in risk of offending than adults (70 per cent compared with 92 per cent).

Persistent offenders were as likely as first or early offenders to be perceived as less at risk of recidivism since being made subject to probation (75 per cent compared with 73 per cent) but probationers convicted of a main offence involving dishonesty were less often thought to have demonstrated a reduction in risk than those convicted of "conduct" or "other" offences (66 per cent compared with 80 per cent and 83 per cent). With breaches excluded, the lack of a difference in this respect between persistent and first or early offenders persisted and the offence related difference disappeared. Overall, women were as likely as men to be perceived as being less at risk of further offending (69 per cent compared with 73 per cent). Taking account only of "successful" probation orders, however, women, it appeared, were slightly less likely than men to have demonstrated a reduced risk of re-offending since being placed on probation (73 per cent compared with 86 per cent).

Only three offenders were considered to be at a greater risk of recidivism than when they received their probation orders. In one case the offender's circumstances had changed for the worse:

"He has moved into a circle of friends who are heavily into anti-social activities. He has also left his mother's home."

Another offender in this category was said to be "getting used to the prison system" while a third, who had subsequently been imprisoned for offences committed prior to being placed on probation was described as being embittered by the experience and had not "changed his attitudes towards women".

Two offenders whose risk of re-offending was believed not to have changed were considered not, in any case, to have presented a risk of further offending when they were made subject to probation. In one case the social worker explained that the "offending was due to special circumstances" while another offender was described as having "already suffered the consequences before being placed on probation". The explanations offered by social workers as to why other offenders' levels of risk had remained unchanged are summarised in Table 4.13.

Table 4.13: Reasons provided by social workers as to why the risk of offending remained the same

	(n=19)
No change in attitudes/behaviour	10
No change in circumstances	6
Alcohol abuse not addressed	2
Continued drug use	1
Offending peer group	1

In ten of the 19 cases in which the risk of offending was thought to have remained the same, this was attributed to no change having occurred in the probationer's attitudes or behaviour. In most cases this was despite the efforts of supervising officers. In three instances, however, social workers acknowledged that little work had been done on offending behaviour. One social worker, for example, explained that the probationer "spent first quarter in prison on sentence, six weeks liberated then remanded and sentenced".

Factors Contributing to a Reduction in Risk

The factors which were believed to have contributed to a reduced risk of further offending are summarised in Table 4.14. The explanations offered by social workers in respect of the two groups of probationers (those who were thought slightly less likely to re-offend and those who were thought much less likely to re-offend) differed in two important respects.

First, they were more likely in the case of probationers who were deemed slightly less at risk of further offending to emphasise in their accounts the possibility of further offending should the offender's circumstances change:

"Should he continue to control his alcohol intake he should not come to the attention of the authorities."

"[The probationer] is maturing, has had a positive period in his life and seen that he can obtain the things he wants legitimately. Employment will be the main deciding factor."

"There is a degree of progress but the other factors in his life militate against him maintaining it."

Second, social workers, in offering accounts of why probationers were significantly less at risk of re-offending, more often made reference to active steps their probationers had taken (dissociating themselves from offending peers) or techniques they had developed to avoid further offending in future:

"Client has developed techniques to control anger. Also has a more positive outlook."

"Did not like the consequences. Is more able to think of other options and avoid choosing 'wrong' choice."

"He acted upon an expressed commitment to avoid offending by making significant changes in his life - one being distancing himself from previous associates."

Table 4.14: Social workers' views as to the reasons for a reduced risk of re-offending

	Slightly less (n=34)	Much less (n=26)
Wish to avoid consequences of further offending	7	6
Increased maturity	6	4
Greater insight into behaviour	5	3
Motivated to change/stop offending	5	5
Alcohol use reduced/under control	5	1
Less impulsive	3	0
Has positive options/outlook	3	2
Drug intake reduced/under control	2	2
Personal relationships/responsibilites	2	3
Employment	2	3
Has made progress	2	0
Circumstances improved	1	0
Has moved to new area	1	0
Stable circumstances	0	6
Has developed techniques to avoid offending	0	4
Better able to cope	0	4
Avoids offending peers	0	4
Reduced stress	0	3
Issues tackled effectively	0	2

The contribution of probation to the reduction of risk

Sixty-eight probationers in total were believed to be less at risk of re-offending since being placed on probation. To what extent was probation, as opposed to other factors, believed to have contributed to the perceived reduction in risk? In almost every case (64 out of 68 or 94 per cent) where the risk of offending was perceived to have reduced, probation was considered to have played some part in achieving that reduction in risk. In 13 cases (19 per cent) it was believed to have played a significant part. More generally, probation was thought to have had some positive impact upon the risk of re-offending in respect of 68 per cent of all probationers in the sample.

SOCIAL WORKERS' COMMENTS ON PROBATION

Social workers were given an opportunity to offer additional comments on individual cases. In nine cases social workers explained that probation had not been the most appropriate disposal, either because of the probationers' circumstances, their lack of motivation or the fact that the order was rapidly breached. For instance:

"Given age, maturity and lack of specific issues - not the most appropriate candidate for such a sentence."

"Due to his attitude it was not possible to carry out effective work."

"Can only be effective if client well motivated to attend for interviews. I do not think he appreciated the seriousness of his position."

"This case never really got off the ground. Quicker assessment for detox and rehab may have been helpful."

Two other social workers explained that their probationer had simply "gone through the motions" of complying with their probation order to avoid a return to court:

"He just did what he had to do to stay out of jail and avoid breach."

"[The probationer] did enough to get through his order but I don't expect much real change in him."

In four cases social workers believed that while probation had not been an appropriate disposal, there were no other more appropriate options available. As one social worker explained:

> "[The probationer is] a vulnerable man - related to mild learning difficulty. I would speculate that statutory involvement via probation not entirely appropriate for someone in [the probationer's] situation although he would likely receive very little support on a voluntary basis from this department as his need could not be viewed as a priority."

Four social workers explained that, although their probationers were now less at risk of offending, this was as much or more to do with other positive changes in their circumstances which could not necessarily be attributed to social work intervention. For example:

> "I don't feel I did much other than point him in a certain direction (which he might have chosen naturally anyway). If he sustains relationship with girlfriend and thereby avoids former 'mates' I think [the probationer] will do all right by himself."

> "Supervision has been influential but the key factor in settling this client has been the routine and responsibilities of employment."

In most cases, however, social workers took the opportunity to highlight the progress made by probationers or the appropriateness of probation in specific cases:

> "Probation seemed to come at the right time in that the client was able to confront her concerns re her increasing stress with regards to caring for her child. As such this gave her the space to concentrate on other things."

> "Probation avoided custody for this ill offender when custody was a real risk and would have aggravated his problems. Joint work with psychiatric services helped assessment and won reluctant co-operation with treatment, besides linking family with a supportive network."

> "I/we were lucky in that we got breaks re housing and employment, but [the probationer] has also positively changed his attitude to theft/offending in general."

> "[The probationer] needed some intervention to help him make sense of his life. Probation provided the vehicle for that intervention."

> "Difficult case. Significantly client progressed from an aggressive, highly stressed individual to one who challenged professionals and authorities in an assertive manner."

SUMMARY AND CONCLUSIONS

Social workers believed that in most respects they and their probationers were broadly agreed as to the main issues in the case. Addressing offending and drug use, providing the probationer with practical support, getting the probationer through or monitoring the order and addressing attitudes or behaviour associated with offending were the objectives of supervision most commonly identified by social workers. The greatest progress was thought to be made towards achieving objectives concerned with personal relationships, offending and successful completion of the order. Around a third of probationers were said to have been very motivated to address their offending and just over a quarter were thought highly motivated to address other problems. Three-fifths of probationers were said to have responded positively to probation. In most instances probationers' responses to probation were believed to have been influenced positively by their desire to avoid offending and its likely consequences or their wish, more generally, to obtain help with other problems. Those aspects of probation which probationers were believed to have found most helpful included having someone to discuss their problems with, obtaining support and making progress in addressing problems. Features of the appointments themselves - their rigidity, frequency or location - were most often mentioned as those aspects of probation which probationers had found least helpful.

Forty per cent of probationers were considered unlikely to re-offend while in 17 per cent of cases re-offending was thought very likely. Perceived risk of re-offending was inversely related to probationers' motivation, their response to probation and the extent to which offending related objectives had been achieved. Probationers were assessed as very likely to re-offend because their attitudes, behaviour or circumstances were unchanged. Social workers placed greater emphasis upon potential circumstances or pressures which might result in further offending in respect of offenders whom they considered fairly likely to re-offend. In discussing probationers who were assessed as unlikely to re-offend, social workers made reference to their motivation to avoid further offending, improvements or stability in their personal circumstances and the acquisition of personal skills.

Just under three-quarters of probationers were considered less likely to re-offend since being placed on probation. Reductions in risk were associated with the probationer's motivation, response to probation and the extent to which offending related objectives were achieved. The risk of re-offending was usually considered to have remained unchanged if there had been no change in the offender's attitudes or circumstances. Where probationers were thought slightly less likely to re-offend, social workers often emphasised the possibility of further offending should the offender's circumstances change. In the case of those who were said to be much less likely to re-offend, reference was more often made to active steps that probationers had taken or skills they had acquired to avoid offending in future. In almost every case in which the risk of re-offending was said to have reduced social workers believed that probation had played some part in reducing the risk. Probation was believed to have had some positive impact upon the risk of re-offending in 68 per cent of cases in the sample.

The objectives identified by social workers varied in some respects across the research sites. Drug and alcohol related objectives were more prevalent in Scott, while social workers in Wallace referred less often to objectives linked to the provision of practical support but more often to those related to employment and relationships. Probation objectives were least likely to be achieved in Wallace and probationers in that area were less often considered to have been motivated to address their offending and other problems and to have responded positively to probation. Wallace probationers were more often thought to present a continued risk of re-offending.

Probation objectives were more often believed to have been achieved in Bruce. Probationers in this area were less likely to be considered at risk of further offending and were more likely to be said to have demonstrated a reduction in risk while subject to probation (reflecting, perhaps, the fact that they were, in general, a less risky group in the first place). The most surprising finding in the present chapter, however, was the apparent emphasis placed by Bruce social workers upon offending related objectives when, as we have seen in the previous two chapters, offending featured less often in this area in the reasons for recommending probation, in action plans, in the services provided to probationers and in the objectives derived from an analysis of case files. The pattern of findings suggests that tackling offending may often have been an implicit objective in Bruce, which was addressed indirectly through attention to other areas. This explanation would be consistent with the argument, developed in the present report, that social workers in Bruce were adopting a different model of supervision from social workers in Scott and Wallace, with the latter placing greater emphasis upon confronting offending behaviour directly and the former focusing instead primarily upon the personal problems experienced by probationers.

The alternative explanation for these apparently contradictory findings - that the researchers failed to identify accurately objectives from case files - is not borne out by the findings in the other two areas. Nor is it substantiated when the objectives of supervision are examined according to the characteristics of individual probationers for, as we shall now see, objectives identified by social workers as having been pursued with different groups of offenders bore a striking similarity to those identified in Chapter Three.

Offending was more likely to feature as an objective of supervision with young offenders while work with adult offenders was more likely to focus upon alcohol abuse and family relationships. Young offenders were considered to have been less motivated to address their offending and other problems or to have shown a positive response to probation. They were more often thought to present a risk of continued offending and were less likely to have demonstrated a reduction in risk of re-offending since being made subject to probation.

As in the previous chapter, offending behaviour was equally likely to feature as an objective in work with first or early and persistent offenders. Providing help in relation to employment, accommodation and financial problems were more often objectives of probation supervision with young offenders, while providing practical support, addressing drug and alcohol abuse and attention to personal relationships featured more often in work with persistent offenders. Probation objectives were less likely to have been achieved with persistent offenders, who were more often thought not to have been motivated to address their offending and other problems. Persistent offenders were less often said to have demonstrated a positive response to probation and were more often thought to present a risk of continued offending. Persistent offenders were, however, as likely as first or early offenders to have shown a reduced risk of re-offending since being placed on probation.

Probation objectives were more likely in the case of probationers who had been sentenced for offences involving dishonesty to relate to addressing offending behaviour and getting the offender through or monitoring the order. Work with "conduct" offenders, on the other hand, was more often said to focus upon alcohol abuse and addressing attitudes or behaviour supportive of offending. The former group of probationers was more often said not to have been motivated to address their offending and were less often thought to have responded positively to probation supervision, though when "successful" cases alone were considered the relationship between type of offence, motivation and response was reversed. "Dishonesty" offenders were more often thought to present a very high risk of further offending and their risk of re-offending was less often thought to have reduced during the period of probation supervision.

Turning, finally, to gender differences, offending behaviour, drug and alcohol use and getting the offender through the order were more likely to feature as objectives of probation supervision with male offenders. By contrast, providing the probationer with practical support and help with financial problems, encouraging personal development and addressing attitudes or behaviour associated with offending were more often cited as objectives of probation practice with women. Women were more often said to have been motivated to address their offending behaviour and other problems and were more often thought to have shown a positive response to probation supervision while men were considered more likely to re-offend. These differences appeared, however, to be attributable to the differing characteristics of male and female probationers in the sample.

Again, therefore, there is evidence of probation practice having been tailored to a substantial degree to the characteristics and perceived needs of different groups of probationers. To the extent that the effectiveness of probation can be assessed with reference to reductions in the risk of recidivism having been achieved, work with young offenders appeared to have been somewhat less successful than work undertaken with older probationers. Supervision of women probationers, however, appeared to be equally effective as supervision of men, and work with persistent offenders as effective in this respect as work with first or early offenders. Objectives pursued in the process of supervision were, however, less often achieved with persistent offenders and in comparison with first or early offenders their relative risk of further offending remained high.

CHAPTER FIVE

PROBATIONERS' EXPERIENCES AND VIEWS OF PROBATION

INTRODUCTION

This chapter explores the perceptions of people on probation, gained from 65 in-depth interviews: 12 in Bruce, 26 in Scott, 4 in Burns, and 23 in Wallace. The sample included a total of 31 adults and 34 young people (aged 16-20 years). It should be noted that questions asked often prompted more than one answer, and therefore total numbers of responses may at times exceed the number of interviewees. The interviews were semi-structured discussions lasting on average between one and one and a half hours and were usually conducted in people's own homes; however, some were held in the local social work offices and 18 in prison. All of those interviewed in custody were from Scott and Wallace, 16 being in custody following breach of their probation orders. Twenty-one interviewees had their probation orders breached, 33 had completed their orders and 11 orders had been discharged early. Fifty-six interviewees were male and nine were female. As such, this group of respondents can be assumed to be broadly representative of the larger sample from which they were drawn.

This chapter of the report assesses the views of probationers against the following benchmarks of National Standards: expectations of probation, action plan, frequency/intensity of contact, intervention and services provided by social workers, offending behaviour and early discharge/breach. The views of probationers on what they would do if they were social workers supervising someone on probation are also considered.

THE PERCEIVED PURPOSE OF PROBATION

When asked what social workers had said would be expected of them on probation at the start of the order, the vast majority of probationers cited the following factors: to keep appointments, not to re-offend and to abide by the rules. Their own perceptions of what was expected on probation were very similar to the views that they assumed social workers held, although many cited in addition a support factor, namely, that they would get help with problems (23 probationers). On the whole, their expectations of probation resulted from previous experience of such a disposal or what they had gleaned from friends, lawyers or the social worker who had been responsible for the preparation of the social enquiry report.

When probationers were asked what disposal they thought they would have received, if they had not been made subject to a probation order, 50 out of 64 respondents (78 per cent) believed that they would otherwise have received a custodial sentence. Fifteen adult and 27 young probationers said they agreed to being placed on probation because they regarded it as a better option than custody. Only a handful had actually reversed their view by the end of the order, suggesting that with hindsight, the majority would still have preferred probation to imprisonment.

When asked what they felt probation was meant to achieve, one of the main purposes - cited by 16 adults and 26 young people - was thought to be to stop people re-offending and to keep them out of trouble. In addition, 17 adults and 20 young people believed that probation was intended to provide people with help with their problems. Whilst many at first perceived the probation order to be essentially a mechanism for the purpose of monitoring and surveillance, some, it appears, had been pleasantly surprised by their experience:

> "When I first went on probation, I thought of them as an open jailer, but at the end I came to think of them more as a friend." (40 year old male)

There appeared to be a general expectation that social workers could and did help people with problems and that this support element should be a significant part of the probation process (see also the section "The Ideal Social Worker" later in this chapter). As one probationer explained:

> "It's not just ten to fifteen minutes in the office once a month. [The social worker] has got to be someone who wants to help." (19 year old male)

This expectation of help contrasts with the pessimistic, but certainly minority, view that probation was purely a monitoring exercise and that the probationer need only "play the game":

> "I thought I'd just go down there and talk a lot of crap and then come back up the road. That's what I done most of the time.... tell them I was off drugs and that." (17 year old male)

The fact that so many probationers perceived probation to be a direct alternative to custody suggests that there could have been an element of "Hobson's Choice" in their agreeing to the making of a probation order in the first place. In other words, some probationers may have agreed to probation, not because they wanted support, but because they wanted to avoid imprisonment. Yet for probation to work effectively, those subject to it need to be motivated to modify or improve their situation. It was therefore interesting that, on reflection, the majority of respondents emphasised the importance of the probationer's motivation to change and their willingness to contribute to the process if probation was to be effective:

"You can only change yourself, nobody else can change you." (17 year old male)

"You can't change a human character just with giving them probation." (32 year old male)

The significance of the probationer's motivation to change in relation to the effectiveness of probation supervision was also, it will be recalled, highlighted in Chapter Four.

One 18 year old summed up the feelings of many when he put himself in the role of a social worker supervising an offender on probation:

"I'd say to [the probationer] there's no point going through with this if you're just going to fuck it up. I'd tell him that straight. I'd say if you're going to stick in and try for yourself, I'll double that effort for you because it does work, I've seen it happen."

THE PROBATION ACTION PLAN

When asked whether they had any knowledge of an action plan being prepared at the start of their order, and how involved they were in drawing it up, the majority of probationers expressed some confusion and many had difficulty distinguishing between the social enquiry report (SER), the probation order itself and the action plan. In Bruce, two-thirds of the interviewees were aware that an action plan had been drawn up, but in Scott around four-fifths of probationers were either unsure of the existence of such a plan or thought an action plan had not been prepared. Similarly in Wallace 20 of the 23 probationers had no recollection of an action plan having been prepared.

This said, all the respondents knew what their social workers believed to be the main issues to be addressed during the period of supervision. Furthermore, probationers believed that, on the whole, the issues which they thought the social worker had identified were compatible with those which they themselves considered relevant and related closely to the problems the probationer was experiencing at that time. The only significant point of divergence related to personal relationships or family problems, with higher priority being attached to these issues by social workers than by probationers: 22 probationers stated that personal and family relationships were highlighted by the social worker whereas only 12 considered them to be significant themselves.

The two most common problems which required to be addressed, and which were thought to be held important by social workers and probationers alike, were offending (identified by 26 social workers and 28 probationers) and the misuse of alcohol or drugs (identified by 14 social workers and 24 probationers). Young offenders were, on average, three times more likely than adult probationers to see offending and problems related to the use of alcohol or drugs as relevant areas to focus upon during the probation order, even though alcohol abuse was more often considered to be an issue with older offenders. This may reflect reluctance on the part of some older offenders to recognise that their alcohol use was problematic and was associated with their offending.

Twenty-six (of 29) adult and 22 (of 32) young probationers indicated that they had been fairly or highly motivated to resolve their personal problems at the point at which the probation order was made. Two adult and 11 young probationers, on the other hand, stated that they had not initially been keen to address their problems. This is consistent with the finding in Chapter Four that young offenders were less often considered by their social workers to have been motivated to address their problems while on probation.

Whilst the majority of probationers could identify issues which both they and the social workers had felt required to be addressed during the order, it may have been additionally helpful if probationers and social workers, at the start of the order, had identified specific goals to be pursued over the period on probation. This would have been a useful tool for monitoring progress or for helping to resolve longer term issues for the probationer. In this respect, reviews - when held - appeared to be useful in the eyes of probationers for receiving acknowledgement of progress made and gaining encouragement and motivation to continue the order successfully. However, the effectiveness of reviews was believed to be dependent upon the identification of clear goals at the outset of the order which could be worked on during the period on supervision.

The lack of an action plan or clear contract of agreement did not seem to deter probationers from addressing problems with their social worker, but this then tended to be done on an ad hoc basis rather than in a structured way. Equally, the lack of an action plan did not adversely affect the respondents' perceptions of the probation process, although it may have affected their perception of its success in helping them to address problem areas, given that they had no real benchmarks against which to monitor their progress.

FREQUENCY/INTENSITY OF CONTACT

Thirty of the 65 respondents felt that the length of their probation order was about right but 22 believed it had been too long, either because of their young age (for example, 16 or 17 year olds getting two year orders), because it had been imposed for a first offence and was seen as too severe a disposal, or because the possibility of breach hung over them throughout the period. As one 18 year old succinctly referred to the threat of breach: "It just gives you more rope to hang yourself".

Most probationers had been informed at the outset that they would have appointments on a weekly basis for the first month, then fortnightly and monthly thereafter. The majority (48 probationers) believed that this level of contact was about right. A few would, depending on their circumstances, have preferred more or less frequent contact overall. Those who were in full-time employment or who were completing community service orders or intensive probation programmes in addition to their probation orders found it difficult to manage their time accordingly. As one probationer explained:

"It was taking two hours off my work and I was in and out in five minutes." (18 year old male)

Several young people in particular would have preferred more contact with their social workers to relieve isolation or boredom:

"It was somewhere to go, someone to talk to." (20 year old male)

Although not a question asked of respondents at interview, approximately a quarter of the probationers commented on the length of appointments. Of those that did, some complained that contacts with their social worker were too short and cursory, suggesting, for example, that social workers, invariably rushed off their feet when the probationer entered the room, would ask a few mundane questions ("How are you?", "How's the job hunting?", "Are you keeping out of trouble?") and then arrange the next appointment. On the other hand, some thought that their appointments were too long (at 30 minutes to an hour in length), given that the probationer might be working or might no longer perceive the need for such intensity of contact.

SOCIAL WORK SUPERVISION AND SUPPORT

In the opinion of probationers, the types of help social workers most often provided were: supporting them with practical or emotional problems (45 probationers); talking and listening to the probationer (43 probationers); and making referrals to or liaising with other agencies (35 probationers). This would accord with the factors which probationers felt to be important in the "ideal" model of social worker (see below), namely, help with practical or emotional problems and talking and listening to the probationer.

The majority of probationers (20 adults and 24 young people) thought that the assistance they had received from their social worker was adequate and that there was nothing further the social worker could have done to help. However, eight probationers would have appreciated additional help in finding a job (two adults and six young offenders), 13 would have valued more support generally (eight adults and five young people) and five (one adult and four young people) would have appreciated more "outings"[51] with the social worker.

Consistent with the findings presented in Chapter Three, the most commonly mentioned agencies to which social workers had referred their probationers provided services in relation to drugs (14), employment or voluntary work (14), medical problems (7), housing (6) and alcohol (5). As previously indicated, 35 probationers commented on the helpfulness of being put in touch with other agencies or having their social worker contact them on their behalf. Coincidentally, the latter approach of advocacy was deemed to be more fruitful as a means of ensuring that the probationer actually made use of the agency - hence the criticism by some probationers that social workers were not directive enough and left the 'running' too much up to the probationer. Young people especially tended to appreciate the social worker taking the lead on occasion in helping them manage their affairs. This should not necessarily be seen as young people refusing to take responsibility for their actions, but rather as a perhaps understandable reaction to what often were perceived as multiplying or insurmountable problems.

In the course of interview probationers were asked to indicate what they had hoped to achieve while on probation and to rate, on a five point scale, the extent to which each of their objectives had been achieved.

---

[51] Outings is an expression many picked up from their experience as children of social work input, but was not usually meant in the traditional sense of visiting other places, so much as meeting with the social worker outwith the formal environs of the office, either for a walk, a coffee or a drive. It was often seen as a better medium for getting to know someone and building trust/confidence in them.

The resultant responses are summarised in Table 5.1. Interestingly, 37 probationers (57 per cent of the interview sample) regarded the avoidance of further offending or addressing their offending behaviour as a key personal objective while on probation.

Table 5.1: Probationers' objectives and the extent to which they were achieved

Objectives	Totally/to a significant extent	Partially	To a limited extent/not at all	Total	Percentage[52] achieved
Offending	28	1	8	37	76%
Employment/education	14	4	11	29	48%
Drug use	10	3	3	16	62%
Stabilise lifestyle	8	4	1	13	61%
Personal development	9	1	3	13	69%
Alcohol use	8	1	2	11	73%
Accommodation	5	3	2	10	50%
Family relationships	3	1	4	8	38
Other practical issues	5	0		7	71
Get through order	4	1	1	6	67
Financial	1	2	3	6	17
Personal relationships	2	1	2	5	40

Significant progress was thought to have been made in a majority of cases in achieving objectives related to the avoidance of further offending; personal development; the control of drug or alcohol use; other practical issues; and maintaining a more stable lifestyle. Progress was more mixed in relation to employment/education and accommodation with objectives thought to have been achieved totally or to a significant extent in around a half of cases. The least progress was reported to have been made in respect of family or personal relationships and financial problems, though the numbers of probationers who advanced these as objectives were so small as to prevent firm conclusions from being drawn from the results.

The social worker's approach

Figure 5.1 attempts to illustrate in diagrammatic form those features of their social worker's approach which probationers found helpful or unhelpful.

Figure 5.1: Helpful and unhelpful features of the social worker's approach

HELPFUL

PRACTICAL

Gave me options
Put things in perspective
Knowledgeable
Influential

Easy to talk to
Calm, relaxed, friendly
Treated me as equal/with respect
A good listener
Tactful/trustworthy
A friend
Straightforward
A motivator

EMOTIONAL

SUPPORT

Inexperienced
Did not understand the problem
Too "empowering"

Domineering
Too busy
Too intrusive
Treated me as a child
Did not care
Unapproachable

SUPPORT

UNHELPFUL

---

[52] Percentage of cases in which the objective was thought to have been achieved totally or to a significant extent.

The relationship established between the social worker and the probationer appeared to be crucial to the success of probation. Several probationers commented on the fact that social workers often supplemented, if not replaced, the support role of parents - "It's like having a mum there" - in that they felt at ease talking to their social worker about their problems. At the same time, they also appreciated the social worker treating them as an equal and with respect

Twelve adults and 16 young people felt that *not* getting on well with their social worker would have put the success of the order in jeopardy: at worst they would have failed to keep appointments and been breached as a result, and at best their presence at appointments would have been merely tokenistic. Few probationers realised that they could request a change of social worker but those who actively tried to do so on account of a clash of personalities stated that their request had been ignored.

The ideal social worker

At the end of the interview, respondents were asked to put themselves in the role of social worker and to comment on how they would work with an offender on probation. Once revulsion at the very thought had dissipated and disbelief had been willingly suspended, most respondents set about this role reversal with an admirable sense of gravity and responsibility, drawing on both their good and bad experiences of social workers and probation, and arriving at what, to them, would in effect be the ideal model.

The majority of respondents took an holistic view of the probationer and his/her needs, stressing the importance of getting to know the person, their lifestyle, family background, current problems and future aspirations. The vast majority did not see this as an intrusion of privacy if it was obvious to the probationer that sharing such information might help to resolve their current problems.

The most commonly mentioned aspect of a "good" social work approach was finding out what the probationers' problems were in an attempt to get to the root causes of their offending (34 respondents); equally important was giving practical help or advice (32), followed by getting to know the probationer as an individual (25), having a friendly, encouraging or caring approach (19) and talking/listening to the probationer (14). Seventeen respondents stressed the importance of the probationer wanting help in the first place before an effective relationship could be established and most highlighted the need to encourage the active involvement of the probationer in the process of change:

> "Let him [the probationer] talk about what he wants to talk about, and not what you want to know." (17 year old male)

OFFENDING BEHAVIOUR

Addressing offending behaviour was recognised by probationers as being an integral and necessary part of probation. The main expectation that probationers had at the outset of their order was that they must not re-offend. The primary purpose of probation was perceived as being to help the probationers to avoid re-offending, and in the ideal model examining the root causes of offending featured highly. Only three probationers did not apparently discuss offending during their period on probation. The majority had discussed offending in some detail with their social worker and ten described exercises on offending behaviour which they had been asked to undertake. Many of those who commented on the content of discussions about their offending behaviour could recite almost verbatim the advice that the social worker had given, in terms of the consequences of their actions or how to stay out of trouble in the future, even though many of them had thought at the time that it would "go in one ear and out of the other".

Probation groups - which tended to run only when staff and financial resources allowed - were generally regarded positively by those probationers who had had experience of them because they found the groupwork element stimulating. Whilst some felt that familiarity with other participants caused problems for them, the majority believed the group discussions and exercises to have been useful and challenging. Attendance at probation groups, more generally, helped to relieve boredom and kept probationers "off the streets".

Intensive Probation Projects (IPPs) - described by one participant as "a criminal version of Alcoholics Anonymous" - operated in three of the areas under study. Eleven respondents in total were involved in an IPP and on the whole did not find the commitment (on average three days a week) too difficult to manage. Indeed many said that they missed the contact once it had finished. Most believed that the intensive probation programme helped them realise how their offending was adversely affecting their lives and appreciated the opportunity and space to talk about their problems and to look at alternative lifestyles.

Sixty-one probationers offered a view as to their continued risk of re-offending. The majority (42) believed it was unlikely that they would re-offend, while 13 thought that further offending was fairly likely and six thought it was very likely. Thirty-nine per cent of young probationers thought it likely that they would re-offend compared with 21 per cent of adults. Each of the four probationers in Burns and all but one in Bruce considered further offending unlikely. By comparison, this was true of just over half the probationers in Wallace and Scott. In 57 cases it was possible to compare the views of social workers and probationers as to the risk of continued offending posed by the latter. Agreement as to the level of risk was found to occur in 30 cases (53 per cent). In five of the remaining cases, probationers considered themselves more at risk of re-offending than did their social workers; in 22 cases probationers thought themselves less at risk of further offending than did the supervising officers.

Compared with when they were placed on probation, just over two-thirds of probationers (45) considered themselves now to be much less likely to re-offend while six others thought they were slightly less likely to commit further offences. Twelve believed themselves to be as much at risk of offending now as they had been when first made subject to probation and one thought that his likelihood of re-offending had significantly increased. Eighty-five per cent of young probationers and 73 per cent of adults believed that they were now less likely to re-offend, though it will be recalled that in Chapter Four young offenders were less often thought by their social workers to have shown a reduction in risk of re-offending while on probation. In 59 cases it was possible to compare probationers' and social workers' views as to the change in risk, if any, that had occurred over the course of probation. In 45 cases the social worker had suggested that the probationer was now less at risk of offending: 38 probationers concurred with this assessment while seven others believed that their risk of re-offending was unchanged. In 13 cases the social worker thought that the risk of further offending remained unchanged: four probationers were of a similar view while nine believed that they were now less at risk of recidivism. In the one case in which the social worker had indicated that the probationer presented a greater risk of re-offending by the time the order was terminated the probationer also believed this to be the case. Overall, probationers and their social workers were agreed in their assessment of relative risk in 73 per cent of cases.

The fifty-one probationers who considered themselves now to be at less risk of re-offending were asked to indicate the extent to which probation, as opposed to other factors, had contributed to this reduction in risk. Twenty-one probationers (41 per cent) considered that being on probation had contributed significantly to reducing their likelihood of re-offending; 23 probationers (45 per cent) believed that probation had made some contribution and seven probationers (14 per cent) thought that probation had had no impact in this respect. Overall, then, it would appear that probation was perceived to have had at least some impact on their risk of re-offending by 69 per cent (44 out of 64) of probationers who were interviewed. Adult probationers were more likely than those under 21 years of age to report that probation had made a significant contribution to their reduced risk of re-offending (56 per cent compared with 27 per cent), supporting the conclusion reached in the previous chapter that probation supervision tended to be more effective with adult probationers.

Social workers had also indicated that they believed probation to have impacted upon offending in a similar percentage of cases. When the views of social workers and probationers were compared in the 38 cases in which this was possible, there was agreement in 33 cases (87 per cent) that probation had contributed to the perceived reduction in risk. In half of these 38 cases opinions differed, however, as to the extent to which probation had contributed to this process. In five of the nine cases in which the social worker believed probation to have contributed significantly to a reduction in risk, the probationer was of a similar view. In the remaining cases the probationers believed that probation had made some contribution (two cases) or none (two cases). In 29 cases social workers had believed that probation had had some impact upon reducing the risk of re-offending and in 14 cases the probationer agreed. Three of the remaining 15 probationers considered probation to have had no impact in this respect while 12 thought that probation supervision had made a significant contribution to their reduced risk of further offending. If anything, therefore, it appears that probationers placed greater significance than did their social workers on the contribution of probation supervision.

Three probationers were unable to identify factors other than probation which had made it less likely that they would re-offend. Forty-three others, however, offered a variety of explanations as to why, other than having been on probation, their risk of further offending had decreased. These are summarised in Table 5.2.

A quarter of this group of offenders emphasised the importance of their own determination to avoid further offending. A desire to avoid the consequences of continued offending for themselves or their families also featured prominently. Several probationers pointed to increased stability in their lives (through, for example, having developed meaningful personal relationships, having obtained employment or access to education or having gained control over former misuse of alcohol or drugs). Seven probationers suggested that the influence of friends was important: four because they had made a conscious effort to distance themselves from offending peers and three because they did not want to let their (non-offending) friends down. One former probationer, finally, suggested that subsequently having been placed on community service had strengthened his resolve to desist from further offending behaviour.

Table 5.2: Why probationers were less likely to re-offend

	Number of cases (n=43)
Motivated to stop offending	11
Impact of offending on family	11
Desire to avoid custody	9
Personal relationships	8
Friends	7
Employment/education	7
Getting older	7
Control over drug use	6
Control over alcohol use	4
Settled lifestyle	4
Family responsibilities	3
Being on community service	1

EARLY DISCHARGE/BREACH

As previously indicated, 21 of the probationers who were interviewed had been breached for non-compliance with their probation orders or for further offending. Those who were breached were not necessarily negative about their experience of probation: ten were generally positive about their experience of probation compared with 11 who expressed more negative attitudes. On the other hand, the majority of those who completed their orders in full or whose order had been discharged early gave generally positive accounts of their probation experience. Only seven of the 44 probationers who successfully completed probation were negative, overall, about the experience.

Early discharge tended to be discussed as an option with the probationer where longer orders were involved and where progress was obviously being made and the probationer was not re-offending. Probationers whose orders had been discharged early were, in the main, happy with the process and reported having felt relieved and encouraged by the decision. In a small number of cases, the probationer did not take up the option of pursuing an early discharge, requesting instead that social work support continue for the period originally stipulated in the order.

Ten of the 21 respondents who were breached had been returned to court following conviction for a further offence. Seven had been breached for failure to report to the supervising officer, three for failure to comply with additional requirements and one for failing to notify the supervising officer of a change of address.

The possibility of breach loomed large in the eyes of those on probation and was seen predominantly as a bone of contention. This said, those who were breached tended to accept the situation, and suggested that the social worker had had no alternative but to take that course of action under the circumstances. However, the majority felt strongly that their views had not been taken into account and that their explanations had been disregarded by the social worker, the community service officer or the court. Probationers complained that they had sometimes not received appointment letters or that there had been some confusion over the number of warnings that had been issued. Their lifestyles (and lack of diaries!) may also have contributed towards their inability to keep appointments:

> "...that was just having loads of appointment times and not kenning what one was for what...just things like that and loss of memory with me being on solvents and battling them." (26 year old male)

Of the 18 interviewees who discussed the experience of being breached, six thought that they had been treated fairly by the social worker and the court and that they were fully to blame for being breached; two were non-commital about the process; and the remaining ten believed it had been inappropriate to pursue breach (either because they had not been forewarned of the social worker's intentions, they had not been given a chance to adapt to the requirements of probation, or they had not been given a fair hearing at the time of the breach being processed). Information about the delay between orders being suspended and the breach being heard at court was not routinely gathered from individual case files. However, the impression gained by the researchers was that lengthy delays often occurred between suspension of an order and the breach being heard in court (a problem which was highlighted, in particular, by social work managers in Bruce). This could result in probationers who were breached finding it difficult to equate the process with the outcome.

OVERALL IMPRESSIONS OF PROBATION

In general, most probationers considered their experience on probation to have been worthwhile and of benefit to them. The features cited as being most helpful included having someone to talk to, having emotional or practical support, being able to focus the mind on options for the future and being able to remain in the community rather than being sent to prison. The features of probation which probationers found least helpful were the possibility of breach (and its concomitant sentence of imprisonment), the frequency or location of appointments, the intrusion into one's privacy and feeling that help with problems was not forthcoming. The views expressed by probationers, therefore, tended to be in accord with social workers' perceptions of what probationers had found most and least helpful about probation supervision.

Problems relating to appointments were mentioned by 12 respondents. Some complained that the frequency of appointments made other commitments (full-time employment, community service, attendance at intensive probation projects) difficult; that appointments were too early in the morning; that the office was inaccessible (too far to walk, no money for bus fares, did not want to be seen in the area by peers/police); or that mental or physical health problems made office visits difficult.

Only five adults and 11 young people stated that they had gained nothing from probation. The remainder cited benefits such as resolving their problems, gaining self-confidence, motivation or self-respect, learning self-control and having "time-out" to reflect on or change their situation.

The majority of probationers (22 adults and 26 young people) felt that the social worker's input had been helpful. However, some felt that the order per se - or, more specifically, the possibility of breach - rather than the social worker's input had influenced their ability to abide by the rules throughout the period of probation. Twelve probationers suggested that the threat of breach was a greater deterrent to re-offending than, for example, analysing offending behaviour.

Some probationers looked to probation to offer, in addition to supervision, an element of structure and control which had been missing from their lives in the past. Equally, many respondents intimated that social workers could fulfil an encouraging and supportive role better than could family or friends: they are older, more experienced, have better contacts and know-how, are neutral outsiders and are there to help:

> "Talking to people outside the situation gives you an estimate of what you're worth in their eyes, which begins to sort of re-establish your values again." (42 year old female)

Very few probationers regarded probation as purely a monitoring exercise. The majority expected their social workers to be proactive in helping them address their problems and expected probation, overall, to be more problem solving than punishing. Whilst 22 probationers believed that tackling offending behaviour should be a key element of the social worker's task, the vast majority thought that the focus of probation should be on problems relating to practical survival and emotional well-being. Offending was invariably seen by probationers as a by-product of such problems - resulting from a lack of money, boredom, pressure from friends or unfair discrimination by, for example, the police.

Although it often took time for probationers to realise the extent of their problems or to get to know and trust their social workers enough to confide in them, such rapport, once established, seemed to be very effective:

> "I don't think I'd have known what to do without him half the time. It was him I first told about my drugs problem, the very first person I told." (17 year old male)

> "...just with [my social worker] talking to me, saying that I was good staying out of trouble for this amount of time. I felt a lot more confident than what I was. I thought I was a loser, the only thing I could do was steal things, but he made me feel a bit more confident in myself." (22 year old male)

One probationer, finally, summed up the benefits to him of having been on probation as follows:

> "This is the first year since I've been took off probation I've no had anything to do with anything any more, no social workers, courts, anything for a while. I've no outstanding, nothing left. It is [a great feeling]. I can walk about the streets now and I don't need to turn my back every two seconds waiting for the polis motoring down. There used to be warrants out for me as well, but I've no any warrants now... I've got a clean bit of paper now." (21 year old male)

SUMMARY AND CONCLUSIONS

Most probationers recognised that one of the main purposes of probation was to address offending behaviour and just over half suggested that it was also intended to provide help with problems. The majority of probationers stressed the importance of being motivated to change and willing to contribute to the process for probation to be effective. Most probationers were unclear about the existence of an action plan, though they were aware of what the social worker considered to be the main issues in the case and were generally in accordance with the social worker's definition of the problem areas to be addressed. Offending behaviour and drug or alcohol problems were most often mentioned by probationers as areas which should be worked on during probation. Three-quarters of probationers indicated that they had been motivated to address their problems when placed on probation; however, in agreement with social workers' views, younger offenders were less likely than adult probationers to be motivated in this respect.

Just under half the probationers thought that the length of their order had been about right while a third believed it to have been too long. Most believed that the frequency of contact with their social worker was about right though a few would have preferred more or less frequent contact, depending upon their circumstances. Probationers identified help with practical or emotional problems, having someone to talk to and referral to/liaison with other agencies as of most benefit to them. Most believed that the help they received from their social workers was adequate, though two-fifths would have valued additional help of a practical or supportive kind. The features of probation which probationers found least helpful were the location or frequency of appointments and the possibility of breach. The relationship established with the social worker appeared to be a significant aspect of probation supervision. Those features of the social worker's approach which probationers found most helpful were openness and approachability combined with an ability to influence circumstances and help the probationer to better understand his/her situation and behaviour.

When asked what they had hoped to achieve while on probation, probationers most often cited avoidance of further offending (in just under three-fifths of cases) followed by employment/education, addressing drug use, obtaining a more stable lifestyle, personal development, addressing alcohol use, and accommodation. To a significant extent, therefore, the objectives identified by probationers were similar to those identified by their supervising social workers. The majority of probationers reported that they had discussed offending behaviour in some detail during their probation order. Those who had attended probation groups or intensive probation programmes generally found such approaches to be stimulating and challenging.

Most probationers believed that it was unlikely that they would re-offend, though further offending was thought more likely by young probationers. Compared with when they were placed on probation, over three-quarters of probationers considered themselves to be less at risk of re-offending and the majority of this group believed that probation had played some part in reducing this risk. If anything, probationers were more inclined than their social workers to stress the role that probation supervision had played in reducing their risk of further offending. Other factors which were said to have impacted positively upon their risk of re-offending included their own motivation to avoid offending and its consequences, and improvements in their personal circumstances. In this regard probationers' views were remarkably similar to those of their supervising social workers.

Overall, most probationers believed that their experience on probation had been worthwhile. While a quarter thought that they had gained nothing from probation, the remainder cited benefits such as resolving their problems, gaining self-confidence, motivation or self respect, learning self-control and having "time out" to reflect on or change their situation. Some wanted not just supervision but an element of control to provide structure in their lives which had been absent in the past.

The views expressed by probationers, therefore, support the conclusion that probation supervision was, in a substantial proportion of cases (and more particularly in the case of older probationers), impacting upon their problems and upon their offending and, in so doing, was assisting their integration into the community. The framework provided by the National Standards - with regard to the frequency of contacts between social worker and probationer, the development of action plans and the convening or regular reviews - appears to provide an appropriate structure within which offending behaviour and other issues can be addressed. Despite the confusion which existed in respect of action plans, probationers were in no doubt that the purpose of probation was first and foremost to address offending behaviour and most had discussed their offending in some detail with their social worker. This would suggest that the introduction of 100 per cent funding and National Standards has succeeded in large measure in re-focusing probation practice such as to enhance its emphasis upon tackling offending behaviour and in this way increase the effectiveness, in the short term at least, of probation supervision.

CHAPTER SIX

THE EFFECTIVENESS OF PROBATION SUPERVISION IN SCOTLAND

INTRODUCTION

With a few notable exceptions (for example, Ford et al, 1992)[53] much of the research into the operation and effectiveness of probation supervision to date has concentrated upon services provided by intensive probation and other specialist or innovative projects (for example, Raynor, 1988; Roberts, 1989; Mair et al, 1994)[54]. Relatively little, by contrast, is known about the effectiveness of services provided in the context of mainstream probation practice (Raynor, 1995)[55]. The present study, by examining the characteristics of offenders sentenced to probation, the nature of probationers' problems, the services provided and the short term outcomes of supervision, provides some indication of those factors which may enhance or contribute to the effectiveness of the probation order. This concluding chapter draws together some of the findings from this research and highlights some of the implications for probation practice in Scotland.

THE IMPACT OF NATIONAL STANDARDS ON PROBATION PRACTICE

The introduction of 100 per cent funding and National Standards for probation was aimed at improving the quality and effectiveness of probation supervision, enhancing its credibility with the courts and thereby encouraging the courts to impose probation orders where it is appropriate to do so. The National Standards identify as greatest priority for probation supervision a) those offenders whose current offending behaviour places them at risk of custody, who have significant underlying problems and who seem likely to re-offend (particularly young adult offenders) and b) repeat offenders with significant underlying problems whose offending history places them at risk of custody even if the offence is trivial.

Social work managers from the four study areas who were interviewed were in agreement that the National Standards had brought about significant improvements in probation practice. National Standards, it was suggested, had led to more assured practice and had enabled staff to better plan and co-ordinate their work. As one manager explained:

> "Previously it wasn't given high priority and it's very unlikely there would have been the same level of attention given to action plans and having regular reviews. In that respect I'm quite convinced that National Standards brought about an increase in quality."

This view was supported by sheriffs from courts in the study areas who expressed greater confidence in probation supervision following the introduction of National Standards partly because they now had a clearer understanding of the framework within which supervision was provided and partly because they believed that probation was now more structured and more focused, with the demands on the probationer more clearly defined (Brown and Levy, 1998).

One potential mechanism for providing increased structure in a probation order is the action plan, which should clearly set out the tasks to be undertaken in the course of probation supervision as agreed with the probationer. Almost all probation orders contained action plans but many probationers were unaware of the existence of a plan and their understanding of the aims of probation appeared to be based more on a shared understanding with their social worker than a formal contractual agreement which specified clearly the proposed purpose and content of supervision. The setting of measurable and achievable goals in the action plan may, however, provide a clearer and more structured framework for probation practice which enables progress to be reviewed and which can serve as a means of offering probationers feedback and reinforcement in a more systematic and meaningful way. As Raynor (1996)[56] has argued, effective programmes of supervision tend to be highly structured, with explicit and clear expectations conveyed to the probationer, and are delivered in a consistent manner with procedures to monitor and maintain "programme integrity" and reduce "drift".

---

[53] Ford, R., Ditton, J. and Laybourn, A. (1992) *Probation in Scotland: Policy and Practice*, Edinburgh: Scottish Office Central Research Unit.

[54] Raynor, P. (1988) *Probation as an Alternative to Custody*, Aldershot: Avebury. Roberts. CH (1989) *Hereford and Worcester Young Offender Project*, Oxford: University of Oxford. Mair, G. et al (1994) *Intensive Probation in England and Wales, Home Office Research Study No. 133*, London: HMSO.

[55] Raynor, P. (1995) *Effectiveness Now*: a personal and selective overview in G. McIvor (ed) *Research Highlights in Social Work No. 26: Working with Offenders* London: Jessica Kingsley.

[56] Raynor, P. (1996) Evaluating probation: the rehabilitation of effectiveness, in T. May and A.A Vas (Eds) *Working with offenders: Issues, Contexts and Outcomes*, London: Sage.

Regular reviews, which are required by the National Standards and which were viewed by social work managers as providing first line managers with an opportunity to monitor ongoing work with probationers, likewise have the potential of providing encouragement and reinforcing the progress made on probation. Their effectiveness could equally be further enhanced by the systematic setting of objectives at the start of the order. Early discharge of the probation order, while not always pursued as an option by the probationer, could, it appeared, similarly serve to positively reinforce the progress that had been achieved.

If the possibility of early discharge served as a "carrot" for some probationers, so did the possibility of breach, for many, serve as a "stick". National Standards were believed by social work managers to have introduced greater clarity regarding the procedures to be adopted in respect of probationers who failed to comply with the requirements of their orders and in the evidential requirements for breach. Whilst one manager believed that there were still considerable variations between staff as regards adherence to and interpretation of National Standards, the more general view was that staff were now more willing to instigate breach proceedings in accordance with the guidance and were more confident in doing so. Such an approach was believed to enhance the credibility of probation both with the courts and with probationers. As one manager in Scott explained:

"If you have a fairly robust disciplinary approach to an offender at the beginning of an order you quite often find that these are the cases whereby the order finishes successfully. If you have a slightly weak and slightly problematic response or varied response to somebody who is not co-operating you find ultimately these are the ones that are actually breached. So I'm trying to say to social workers, if you are wanting to be more liberal, paradoxically you should be firmer and tougher, particularly at the outset of an order and that pays dividends...Since National Standards we haven't lost one breach yet, there hasn't been one. There have been general comments [from fiscals] that at the early stages it was slightly unclear why we were breaching somebody...Also the sheriffs were slightly concerned as to why we were breaching somebody but recommending continuation of a probation order...and there was an element of communication which had to take place with regard to these things. This is by and large over because the sheriffs are now fully aware of why we do this and the fiscals are now too."

The present study did, indeed, reveal that in the vast majority of cases breach proceedings were being instigated by social workers following a maximum of two formal warnings as stipulated by the National Standards. This being the case, it was a source of frustration to social work staff, particularly in the authority in which Bruce was located, that lengthy delays were often encountered in the processing of breaches by the court. Thus, according to one manager:

"I think it has made social workers much more likely to breach sooner than they ever would...It started with CSO and I think social workers are now quite committed to the idea of breaching people early if they haven't got good reasons for not doing it, whereas in days gone by it was a last resort...The social workers are extremely frustrated because they are doing all this National Objectives and Standards and the courts can't handle their end of it."

For those probationers who were returned to court in breach of their probation order, whether for failure to comply with the requirements or as a consequence of further offending during the currency of the order, the delay between suspension of the order and the court hearing left some somewhat embittered by the process and unable to fully equate the initial reasons for suspension with the eventual outcome. A quicker response to breach applications by procurators fiscal and by the courts may serve to bring home more effectively to probationers - and not just to those who are subject to breach proceedings - the consequences of failing to comply with a probation order.

A further difficulty that was said by managers to have been encountered in some of the study areas - and one which was believed might similarly undermine the credibility of the probation order - related to the monitoring of additional requirements and, in particular, ensuring that specialist agencies, such as mental health professionals or substance abuse counselling services, were operating within the framework of National Standards with respect to enforcement. Each of the study authorities had been engaged in dialogue with other service providers which had served to open up improved communication and had led to greater consistency in this respect.

In general it would appear that the National Standards provide a more structured and more effective framework for probation supervision through requiring that action plans be developed in individual cases, through specifying the frequency of contacts required in the early stages of an order and through requiring that progress and tasks be regularly and systematically reviewed. It has also been shown, however, that with respect to the timing of initial contacts with probationers, the frequency and location of contacts during the initial stage of supervision and the timing of initial reviews, National Standards were not being met in a significant proportion of cases. Social work managers acknowledged that, in terms of adherence to the National Standards, the greatest difficulty had been encountered in achieving the required number of contacts - usually as a result of the probationer's failure to keep appointments - and in meeting certain time-scales. The latter was believed to present particular problems in rural areas where it was suggested, for example, that more efficient use might be made of staff time by arranging several appointments in a given area on the same day, even if this meant in some cases exceeding the time-scales stipulated in the National Standards.

The National Standards, whilst encouraging social workers to adopt approaches to probation supervision which are more likely to address offending behaviour effectively, provide a framework for practice rather than specifying in any precise terms what the content of supervision should involve. Those features of probation supervision which appeared to contribute to its effectiveness, at least in the short term, will be considered later in this chapter. First, however, variations in the process and outcomes of probation across the study areas will be discussed and the impact of local factors on probation practice will be explored.

THE IMPACT OF LOCAL FACTORS ON PROBATION PRACTICE

From the findings presented in Chapter Two it is clear that considerable variation existed across the research sites in terms of the characteristics of offenders who were made subject to probation supervision by the courts. Bruce contained a slightly lower proportion of young offenders, a higher proportion of female probationers, more first offenders and fewer persistent offenders and probationers in Bruce were less often considered by social workers to have been at risk of custody when their probation orders were imposed. Probationers in Wallace had most previous convictions while those in Scott were most likely previously to have served a custodial sentence.

The effectiveness research literature highlights the importance of targeting supervision and services upon offenders who are assessed as presenting a higher risk of re-offending (Andrews, 1995;[57] Andrews et al., 1990[58]; McGuire and Priestley, 1995[59]; McIvor, 1990[60]; Raynor et al, 1994).[61] To the extent that the National Standards prioritise for probation supervision young adult and persistent offenders who might otherwise attract a custodial sentence and who are likely to present a risk of further offending, there was less evidence of appropriate targeting in Bruce. Furthermore, social workers in Bruce were more likely to recommend the attachment of additional requirements to probation orders and Bruce probationers were as likely as those in the other study areas to receive probation orders with additional requirements (usually community service) attached, even though they were less often thought to be at risk of custody. In this respect, effective gate-keeping mechanisms to avoid the use of unnecessarily restrictive measures and to prevent "tariff escalation", appeared not to be in place. Probation orders which carried additional requirements were more likely to be terminated by breach. This is likely to reflect at least partly the characteristics of probationers upon whom additional requirements were imposed. However, it is also possible that the attachment of additional requirements per se increases the risk of non-compliance on account of the additional demands placed upon probationers. Probationers who were interviewed made reference to the demands which additional requirements, such as community service or attendance at intensive probation programmes, placed upon them. Such demands were felt particularly acutely by probationers who were, in addition, in full-time employment.

Of the four study areas, Bruce also appeared to have made least progress towards meeting standards with respect to the frequency of contact with probationers and the timing of initial contacts and reviews. This may in part be a reflection of the particular difficulties encountered in providing services in rural areas. It may also, however, be indicative of antipathy which was said to exist on the part of social work staff towards the guidance contained in the National Standards. Resistance against the concept of National Standards by social workers in Bruce may also account for their apparent adherence to a more traditional "welfare" model of probation supervision, where the offender's problems rather than the offending behaviour itself provides the primary focus for intervention.

The model of probation practice evident in Bruce appears to reflect organisational arrangements in that authority. Although services were delivered by specialist teams, generic management arrangements prevailed at the local level. With criminal justice planning and co-ordination functions centralised and separated from operational responsibilities, there was little opportunity for senior managers to monitor adherence to National Standards and to impact directly upon practice at the local level. Broadly similar organisational arrangements

57 Andrews, A. (1995) The psychology of criminal conduct and effective treatment, in J. McGuire (Ed.) *What Works: Reducing Re-Offending*, London: Wiley.

58 Andrews, A., Zinger, I., Hoge, R.D., Bonta, J., Gendreau, P. and Cullen, F.T. (1990) Does correctional treatment work? A clinically relevant and psychologically informed met-analysis, *Criminology*, 28, 3, 369-404.

59 McGuire, J. and Priestley, P. (1995) Reviewing 'what works': past, present and future, in J. McGuire (Ed.) *What Works: Reducing Re-offending*, London: Wiley.

60 McIvor, G. (1990) *Sanctions for Serious or Persistent Offenders: A Review of the Literature*, Social Work Research Centre, University of Stirling.

61 Raynor, P., Smith, D. and Vanstone, M. (1994) *Effective Probation Practice*, London: MacMillan.

existed in Scott where, in addition, criminal justice social work services were provided by staff in split posts, yet standards were being more consistently met in that area and staff appeared to be more clearly operating within the model of probation practice advocated by the National Standards. In Scott, however, specialist planning and co-ordinating functions had been devolved to the local level and, though having no direct operational management responsibilities in respect of area team staff, the manager responsible for planning and co-ordination instituted a system of regular sampling of SERs and probation, throughcare and community service cases - the results of which were fed back to social work teams - as a means of monitoring adherence to National Standards and improving the quality of practice.

Split posts per se did not, therefore, appear to have adversely influenced the ability of social workers to operate according to the guidance contained in National Standards, though the necessity of undertaking, in addition to criminal justice work, other social work tasks - and, in particular, those relating to child protection - was acknowledged to place an extra strain on social work staff. Fully specialist arrangements for the provision of social work services in the criminal justice system were introduced, but to maintain a decentralised service this resulted in very small numbers of specialist staff in area teams. Problems arose in maintaining practice in accordance with the National Standards when staff shortages (through staff turnover or illness) occurred, and split posts were subsequently re-introduced. Although there was no evidence that practice was any less effective in Scott than in other areas (and, indeed, it may have been more effective in some respects) less use appeared to be made in this area than in Burns and Wallace - both of which had specialist arrangements to at least middle management level - of a range of "off the peg" programmes and materials aimed at addressing offending behaviour and underlying attitudes. It is possible, therefore, that the additional pressures created by split posts, through conflicting demands on staff time, may have prevented the introduction of more innovative methods of work.

Another factor which influenced practice at the local level was the range of other services which existed and which could, therefore, be drawn upon in developing packages of probation supervision. The nature of additional requirements, for example, tended to reflect the availability of locally based resources. The greatest difficulty in accessing a range of other services was said to occur in Bruce since, although the authority in which it was based had traditionally made extensive use of independent sector provision and continued to do so, the majority of services were based in the city and, even if they ostensibly were available across the entire authority, in practice they were said by managers to be difficult to access by offenders resident in the outlying rural areas. Even in those areas where specific resources were available, independent sector providers commented upon the effort required, through regular contact with social work teams, to ensure a consistent flow of referrals.

Scott made the least use of services provided by the independent sector, primarily because the majority of services, such as intensive probation for high tariff offenders, were provided directly by the local authority. Relationships between the local authorities and the independent sector were reported to be good and were thought to have improved since the creation of specialist arrangements for service delivery. In Burns, however, substance abuse counselling agencies - which normally offered services only on a voluntary basis - had been resistant to making available a court mandated service and, in particular, to assuming the associated responsibilities for enforcement which this required. Whilst one agency decided to employ designated staff with a specific remit, to enable them to provide a statutory service to the courts, little progress had been made in resolving this issue with another organisation. As such, social workers were unable to recommend to the courts the imposition of additional requirements relating to drug treatment which they could guarantee would be rigorously and appropriately enforced.

THE SHORT TERM EFFECTIVENESS OF PROBATION SUPERVISION

Probation supervision was viewed by most probationers as helpful and there was some evidence of an improvement in the social circumstances of some offenders following their period on probation, though this could not necessarily be attributed to the impact of social work intervention per se. On the other hand, social workers and probationers were in concurrence that probation supervision had contributed to a reduced risk of re-offending in around two-thirds of cases. Other factors which appeared to have lessened the risk of further offending included increased stability and improved social circumstances in probationers' lives. However, significant reductions in the perceived risk of offending also appeared to be linked to the probationer's acquisition of skills which would help them avoid, or deal more appropriately with, situations which might otherwise place them at risk of further offending behaviour.

The findings also point to the significance of the offender's own motivation to avoid further offending and to address other problems, a feature which was highlighted by Ford et al. (1992). Increased motivation - as assessed by social workers - was associated with reductions in risk, and personal motivation to change was stressed by probationers themselves as a key factor in avoiding further offending and its consequences. Some probationers, it would appear, were clearly not motivated from the outset to examine and change their lifestyles. For some, the benefits to be gained from pursuing an offending-free lifestyle may not have been great enough or accessible enough to outweigh the rewards to be accrued, in the short term at least, from a continued offending career. For others, outstanding charges and the possibility of receiving a custodial sentence, despite their best efforts on probation, may have served as a disincentive to use probation constructively as a vehicle for change. Assessment of motivation would, therefore, appear to be critical at the pre-sentence stage in determining the appropriateness of probation supervision in individual cases. Consent to an order in itself is not necessarily indicative of such motivation since consent will in many cases have been prompted by the understandable desire to avoid a custodial sentence without any necessary wish on the part of the offender to avail him or herself of the assistance and support that probation can provide. In cases such as these, community service might be a more appropriate and, perhaps, more realistic option.

Probationers also highlighted the importance of the relationship established with their supervising social worker as a means of encouraging, supporting and enabling change. While most probationers described their relationship with the social worker in positive terms, few were aware that they could request a change of social worker if the relationship was not working well and those who did request such a change tended, they said, to be ignored. It is important, therefore, that social work departments recognise the potential significance of the social worker-probationer relationship and are both responsive to requests for change and convey clearly to the probationers the fact that such an option exists.

Younger probationers in particular appeared to value the structure that a probation order could provide to enable them to begin to address the multiplicity of problems which many faced. Groupwork provision - whether in the context of an intensive probation programme or mainstream provision - appeared to be viewed positively by probationers as a means of gaining a better understanding of the impact of their offending on themselves and others and exploring alternative options. The majority of supervision was, however, undertaken on an individual basis and in this respect practice would appear not to have changed significantly since the advent of National Standards (see Ford et al., 1992). Although they believed that there had been a general improvement in probation practice since the introduction of 100 per cent funding and National Standards, some social work managers questioned whether the work undertaken with probationers was as effective as it might be. Given that the emphasis had been, on the whole, upon one-to-one work, some managers believed that insufficient attention was still being devoted to addressing offending behaviour:

"What we're finding is that some of them are still not really doing anything other than run of the mill supervision...What we probably don't have yet is a very structured approach to using techniques systematically. Some of the staff say we don't have time basically to do that which implies that we need more staff to do it."

"Social workers are a wee bit weaker in terms of dealing with offending behaviour - they're weakest when they are dealing with, challenging people with their offending behaviour and trying to understand the pattern of offending...If you have a client who has other problems - drug problems or relationship problems or mental health problems - [practice is] extremely good and extremely thorough and these are still essential issues in terms of dealing with somebody on probation."

Whilst there was evidence of use being made in a number of cases of offence focused programmes and other structured methods of intervention (such as anger management techniques) on a one-to-one basis, and while groupwork may be a less effective method of intervention for some offenders, there would appear to be some scope for greater and more imaginative use of groupwork programmes in the context of mainstream probation practice, particularly with young offenders with whom current probation practice still appears to meet with the least success (see Ford et al., 1992) but for whom the peer group constitutes an important reference point and can serve as a powerful vehicle for change, enabling them more quickly to "grow out of crime" (Rutherford, 1986)[62].

One authority - Wallace - had dedicated groupwork provision for sex offenders while one other - Burns - had a probation programme for domestic violence offenders. Three of the four study areas - Burns, Scott and Wallace - had access to intensive probation provision. Otherwise, offence focused work tended to be undertaken on a one-to-one basis. The small numbers of particular categories of offenders, particularly in more rural areas, was said by managers to militate against the development of offence specific groupwork programmes, suggesting the need for more flexible methods of service delivery such as the modular approach.

It was, however, encouraging to find that the probation packages put together by social workers tended to reflect the different reasons underlying the offending behaviour and the differing needs of various categories of probationer. It was also encouraging to observe that probation could, apparently, impact equally upon persistent and first or early offenders, even if the deep-rooted problems experienced by many of the former could less easily be resolved in full within the period of probation supervision and their risk of further offending

---

62 Rutherford, A. (1986) *Growing Out of Crime: Society and Young People in Trouble*, Harmondsworth: Penguin.

remained comparatively high. As far as could be discerned from the available data, probation also appeared to be equally effective with male and female probationers, despite the lesser emphasis placed by social workers on addressing offending behaviour in the context of work with women probationers. To the extent that the present study has demonstrated how probation packages for women probationers differed from those developed for men, the findings are in accordance with those of Stewart et al. (1994) but fail to replicate Ford et al.'s (1992) finding that gender was not a relevant factor in the process and outcomes of supervision. A comparison of the findings from the present study with those of Ford et al. would appear to suggest that, in general, probation supervision has become more clearly focused upon and relevant to the needs of individual probationers and that probationers are, overall, now receiving a better quality of service.

CONCLUSION

In conclusion, the present research presents a generally optimistic picture of probation supervision in Scotland. In the absence of a comparison with practice prior to the introduction of National Standards and 100 per cent funding it is difficult to quantify in any precise terms the impact, in terms of the effectiveness of probation supervision, that the policy has made. Ford et al.'s (1992) study, for example, did not examine the impact of probation upon perceptions of risk. The National Standards and Objectives do appear to provide an appropriate framework for the development of effective probation practice. Combined with the introduction of 100 per cent funding and the associated creation of specialist arrangements for service delivery and with our increased understanding of what approaches are most likely to be effective in working with offenders, the Standards appear to have provided a focus for probation supervision which was largely absent in the past. Probationers were found to be generally clear about the purposes of probation and what it was intended to achieve and were in most instances motivated to address both their offending behaviour and other problems which might be related directly or indirectly to that behaviour. Social workers and probationers appeared to be in general agreement as to the issues that needed to be addressed, even if these were not articulated explicitly and systematically in a probation contract, and probationers and social workers were in agreement that probation could help to alleviate probationers' social and personal problems, assist their integration into the community and contribute to a reduced risk, if not complete cessation, of offending behaviour in a substantial proportion of cases. Probationers were, in general, more optimistic than social workers about the risk of continued offending behaviour. Such optimism, even if it is in some cases misplaced, may be necessary as a first step towards the possibility of sustaining longer term change.

ANNEX I

INFORMATION FROM CASE FILES

The types of information collected from the social work case files of all probationers in the sample were as follows:

- the characteristics of the offender (including age, gender, marital status, living arrangements, employment status, previous criminal history[63]).

- details of the offence/s in respect of which the probation order was imposed (including the number of offences, the nature and gravity rating of the main offence, the form of continuation, and the sentencing court).

- the social worker's assessment of the risk of custody, the recommendation contained in the Social Enquiry Report (SER) and, where relevant, the reasons for recommending probation.

- social and personal problems identified by social workers in SERs and explanations of offending advanced by social workers in these reports.

- details of the probation order made (including length of order and the nature of any additional requirements).

- the reason for termination of the order and the social circumstances of probationers on termination (including accommodation and living arrangements).

---

[63] The Scottish Criminal Record Office provided details of previous convictions to ensure that this information was comprehensive and consistent across study areas.

ANNEX II

INFORMATION FROM CASE FILES (SUB-SAMPLE)

The following information was collected from the social work case files of probationers who were included in the more detailed examination of the process and outcomes of probation supervision:

- the frequency, nature and location of interviews with the probationer.

- the frequency, outcomes and composition of reviews.

- areas of work identified in action plans and during the course of supervision.

- services made available to the probationer, including the method of intervention (individual or group) and by whom services were provided.

- services provided by intensive probation programmes.

- the outcomes of applications to amend requirements and applications for early discharge.

- the number of supervising social workers and reasons for any changes in supervisor.

- the number of formal warnings issued, grounds for breach applications and their outcomes.

- the numbers, types and court outcomes of new offences committed during the period of probation supervision.

ANNEX III

SOCIAL WORKERS' QUESTIONNAIRE

The questionnaires completed by social workers in respect of individual probationers sought their views as to:

- the main areas of work in the case as defined by the social worker and by the probationer.

- the objectives of probation and the extent to which they had been achieved.

- the probationer's motivation to address his/her offending and other problems.

- the probationer's response to probation and factors which had influenced that response.

- the features of probation which probationers had found most and least helpful.

- the risk of continued offending and any change in risk since being placed on probation.

- where relevant, the contribution that probation supervision, as opposed to other factors, had made to achieving a reduction in risk.

Social workers were also invited to offer any other comments about the effectiveness of probation supervision in that particular case.

ANNEX IV

INTERVIEWS WITH PROBATIONERS

The issues addressed in interviews with probationers were as follows:

- why probationers agreed to be placed on probation, their understanding of what probation would involve and what alternative sentence they believed their order had replaced.

- the development of the probation action plan and probationers' involvement in that process.

- probationers' perceptions of the purpose of probation and what it was supposed to achieve.

- problems experienced by probationers, their motivation to address them and the help they received.

- motivation to address offending, whether and how it was discussed by the social worker and the impact of such discussion on probationers' understanding of their offending and their motivation not to re-offend.

- the nature of any additional requirements, what they were supposed to achieve and how helpful they were.

- the frequency and length of contact with the social worker, the relationship established with the social worker and the social worker's approach.

- reasons for any non-compliance or breach and, where relevant, probationers' responses to having been breached.

- where relevant, the appropriateness of early discharge and the probationer's involvement in the decision to seek an early discharge of the order by the court.

- general views about the experience of probation and its effectiveness, including what respondents had hoped to achieve while subject to probationer supervision and the extent to which these expectations were fulfilled.

- views about further offending including the risk of further offending, whether that risk had changed since being placed on probation and, if it had, the contribution that probation supervision, as opposed to other factors, had made to achieving a reduction in risk. Where relevant, probationers were also asked to indicate what other factors had made it less likely that they would re-offend.

REFERENCES

Andrews, A. (1995) The psychology of criminal conduct and effective treatment, in J. McGuire (Ed.) *What Works: Reducing Re-Offending*, London: Wiley.

Andrews, A., Zinger, I., Hoge, R.D., Bonta, J., Gendreau, P. and Cullen, F.T. (1990) Does correctional treatment work? A clinically relevant and psychologically informed meta-analysis, *Criminology*, 28, 3, 369-404.

Brown, L. and Levy, L. (1998) *Social Work Services and Criminal Justice: Sentencer Decision Making*. Edinburgh: The Stationery Office.

Brown, L., Levy, L. and McIvor, G. (1998) *Social Work and Criminal Justice: The National and Local Context*. Edinburgh: The Stationery Office.

Creamer, A., Ennis, E. and Williams, B. (1993) *The Dunscore: A method for predicting risk of custody within the Scottish context and its use in social enquiry practice*, Dundee: Department of Social Work, University of Dundee.

Duffee, D.E. and Clark, D. (1985) The frequency and classification of the needs of offenders in community settings, *Journal of Criminal Justice*, 13, 243-68.

Ford, R., Ditton, J. and Laybourn, A. (1992) *Probation in Scotland: Policy and Practice*, Edinburgh: Scottish Office Central Research Unit.

Mair, G., Lloyd, C., Nee, C. and Sibbitt, R. (1994) Intensive Probation in England and Wales: An Evaluation, *Home Office Research Study No. 133*, London: HMSO.

McAra, L. (1998) *Social Work and Criminal Justice: Early Arrangements*. Edinburgh: The Stationery Office.

McAra, L. (1998a) *Social Work and Criminal Justice: Parole Board Decision Making*. Edinburgh: The Stationery Office.

McIvor, G. (1990) *Sanctions for Serious or Persistent Offenders: A Review of the Literature*, Social Work Research Centre, University of Stirling.

McIvor, G. (1992) *Sentenced to Serve: The Operation and Impact of Community Service by Offenders*, Aldershot: Avebury.

McIvor, G. (1995) Recent developments in Scotland, in G. McIvor (Ed.) *Research Highlights in Social Work No. 26: Working with Offenders*, London: Jessica Kingsley.

McIvor, G. and Barry, M. (1998a) *Social Work and Criminal Justice: Community Based Throughcare*. Edinburgh: The Stationery Office.

McGuire, J. and Priestley, P. (1995) Reviewing 'what works': past, present and future, in J. McGuire (Ed.) *What Works: Reducing Re-offending*, London: Wiley.

Paterson, F. and Tombs, J. (1998) *Social Work and Criminal Justice: The Impact of Policy*. Edinburgh: The Stationery Office.

Raynor, P. (1988) *Probation as an Alternative to Custody*, Aldershot: Avebury.

Raynor, P. (1995) Effectiveness now: a personal and selective overview, in G. McIvor (Ed.) *Research Highlights in Social Work No. 26: Working with Offenders*, London: Jessica Kingsley.

Raynor, P. (1996) Evaluating probation: the rehabilitation of effectiveness, in T. May and A.A. Vass (Eds.) *Working with Offenders: Issues, Contexts and Outcomes*, London: Sage.

Raynor, P., Smith, D. and Vanstone, M. (1994) *Effective Probation Practice*, London: MacMillan.

Rifkind, M. (1989) Penal policy: the way ahead, *The Howard Journal of Criminal Justice*, 28, 81-90.

Roberts, C.H. (1989) *Hereford and Worcester Young Offender Project: First Evaluation Report*, Oxford: Department of Social and Administrative Studies, University of Oxford.

Rutherford, A. (1986) *Growing Out of Crime: Society and Young People in Trouble*, Harmondsworth: Penguin.

Social Work Services Group (1991) *National Objectives and Standards for Social Work Services in the Criminal Justice System*, Edinburgh: The Scottish Office.

Social Work Services Group (1993) *Social Work Services in the Criminal Justice System: Summary of National Objectives and Standards*, Edinburgh: The Scottish Office.

Stewart, G. and Stewart, J. (1993) *Social Circumstances of Younger Offenders Under Supervision*, London: Association of Chief Officers of Probation.

Stewart, J., Smith, D. and Stewart, G. (1994) *Understanding Offending Behaviour*, Harlow: Longman.

04299101   Printed in Scotland for The Stationery Office Limited
                        J37711, C7, 2/98, CCN 003808